1,000,000 Books

are available to read at

www.ForgottenBooks.com

Read online
Download PDF
Purchase in print

ISBN 978-1-332-42276-0
PIBN 10425042

This book is a reproduction of an important historical work. Forgotten Books uses
state-of-the-art technology to digitally reconstruct the work, preserving the original format
whilst repairing imperfections present in the aged copy. In rare cases, an imperfection in
the original, such as a blemish or missing page, may be replicated in our edition. We do,
however, repair the vast majority of imperfections successfully; any imperfections that
remain are intentionally left to preserve the state of such historical works.

Forgotten Books is a registered trademark of FB &c Ltd.
Copyright © 2018 FB &c Ltd.
FB &c Ltd, Dalton House, 60 Windsor Avenue, London, SW19 2RR.
Company number 08720141. Registered in England and Wales.

For support please visit www.forgottenbooks.com

1 MONTH OF FREE READING

at

www.ForgottenBooks.com

By purchasing this book you are eligible for one month membership to ForgottenBooks.com, giving you unlimited access to our entire collection of over 1,000,000 titles via our web site and mobile apps.

To claim your free month visit:
www.forgottenbooks.com/free425042

* Offer is valid for 45 days from date of purchase. Terms and conditions apply.

English
Français
Deutsche
Italiano
Español
Português

www.forgottenbooks.com

Mythology Photography **Fiction**
Fishing Christianity **Art** Cooking
Essays Buddhism Freemasonry
Medicine **Biology** Music **Ancient Egypt** Evolution Carpentry Physics
Dance Geology **Mathematics** Fitness
Shakespeare **Folklore** Yoga Marketing
Confidence Immortality Biographies
Poetry **Psychology** Witchcraft
Electronics Chemistry History **Law**
Accounting **Philosophy** Anthropology
Alchemy Drama Quantum Mechanics
Atheism Sexual Health **Ancient History**
Entrepreneurship Languages Sport
Paleontology Needlework Islam
Metaphysics Investment Archaeology
Parenting Statistics Criminology
Motivational

PS
3504
H87P7
1910

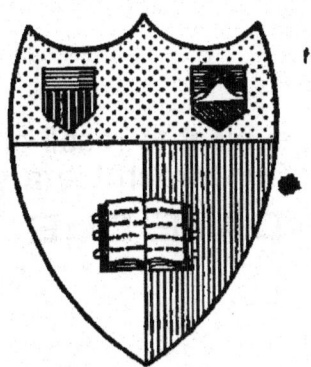

Cornell University Library
Ithaca, New York

FROM

INDIANA PUBLISHER
COMPANY

Cornell University Library
PS 3509.H87P7 1910

The poems of Max Ehrmann.

3 1924 022 384 113   ohn

All books are subject to recall after two weeks.
Olin/Kroch Library

DATE DUE

ned, unconventional and individual verse of re-
al stardust. —PITTSBURG GAZETTE TIMES.

charm of the beautiful mind that created these
beauty in everything he writes. It is a striking
it stamps the author as a poet of genius and ori-
—TRENTON (N. J.) TIMES.

ling, and uniformly high-souled and nobly veined.
—THE BOOK NEWS MONTHLY, (Philadelphia)

derful originality and earnestness. A notable
—KANSAS CITY STAR.

ple, beautiful and straight from the serious part
largeness about this volume, a sweep of express-
f experience, and life is here viewed as from a
—SCRANTON TIMES.

prose-poems, rich in epigrams. Max Ehrmann is
oetry he has no living superior and indeed very
—CHARLESTON (S. C.) NEWS COURIER.

ble feature. —DETROIT NEWS.

of the printed page that Max Ehrmann excels.
gh desire to rid the laborer of oppressions and
Original, unique, and breathing a spirit of rest-
every reader's heart. "A Woman Rocking Her
autiful idea, presented in a setting that only a
—CHARLESTON (S. C.) NEWS COURIER.

ok is "The Light of the Sun," a dramatic work
beauty, and in the part "The Garden of Love"
f delicate sentiment and tenderness. There is
a musical radiance and metrical charm which is
—BUFFALO COURIER.

e will find its pages move and thrill him.
—LOWELL (Mass.) COURIER-CITIZEN.

—PITTSBURG PRESS.

raceful, and ought to live
—THOMAS WENTWORTH HIGGINSON.

e, no meter in the sense of regular recurrence
form has not come from carelessness, for the
oice of words and in accents, so that the lines
sweep that carries the mind on with an irres-
hings. It is the poetry which suggests in its
They are stirring, inspiring, and awake the
hiefly which should bring fame to the poet by
their purpose. An important contribution to
—TERRE HAUTE TRIBUNE.

for himself in untried paths. Nowhere does
ster. He gives the world his own thoughts.
—LEAVENWORTH TIMES.

ssioned, unconventional and individual verse of re-
re real stardust. —PITTSBURG GAZETTE TIMES.

the charm of the beautiful mind that created these
rous beauty in everything he writes. It is a striking
ver it stamps the author as a poet of genius and ori-
—TRENTON (N. J.) TIMES.

f feeling, and uniformly high-souled and nobly veined.
—THE BOOK NEWS MONTHLY, (Philadelphia)

wonderful originality and earnestness. A notable
—KANSAS CITY STAR.

, simple, beautiful and straight from the serious part
e is a largeness about this volume, a sweep of express-
nge of experience, and life is here viewed as from a
—SCRANTON TIMES.

ophic prose-poems, rich in epigrams, Max Ehrmann is
rose-poetry he has no living superior and indeed very
—CHARLESTON (S. C.) NEWS COURIER.

t notable feature. —DETROIT NEWS.

opist of the printed page that Max Ehrmann excels.
high desire to rid the laborer of oppressions and
ns. Original, unique, and breathing a spirit of rest-
cho in every reader's heart. "A Woman Rocking Her
ely beautiful idea, presented in a setting that only a
—CHARLESTON (S. C.) NEWS COURIER.

the book is "The Light of the Sun," a dramatic work
rvelous beauty, and in the part "The Garden of Love"
full of delicate sentiment and tenderness. There is
s and a musical radiance and metrical charm which is
—BUFFALO COURIER.

terature will find its pages move and thrill him.
—LOWELL (Mass.) COURIER-CITIZEN.

song. —PITTSBURG PRESS.

ons, graceful, and ought to live
—THOMAS WENTWORTH HIGGINSON.

t rhyme, no meter in the sense of regular recurrence
ess of form has not come from carelessness, for the
ed in choice of words and in accents, so that the lines
a long sweep that carries the mind on with an irres-
great things. It is the poetry which suggests in its
Bible. They are stirring, inspiring, and awake the
poems chiefly which should bring fame to the poet by
uty and their purpose. An important contribution to
d. —TERRE HAUTE TRIBUNE.

arlessly for himself in untried paths. Nowhere does
g a master. He gives the world his own thoughts.
—LEAVENWORTH TIMES.

Pronouncing the philosophy back of every movement f of mankind.
—ST.

In this volume of poems the author of "A Prayer" has gi as beautiful in sentiment and as simple in language as that made him well known.
—PITTS

It is not ordinary, and its spirituality and force grow u tinued reading.
—LOS

A noteworthy collection.

This is a thoughtful book for thoughtful people. There the thoughts expressed and much spirituality. Among so man it is hard to choose—beautiful enough to be repeated frequen repeated in churches.
—BRO

AN

The volume is a reflection of Max Ehrmann, the man, worth knowing and loving, and it should make him many fri read this delightful volume will recognize the true poet and a among the rare few gifted with the poet's art.
—GRAND

His frankness may provoke censure from some persons knowledge of worldliness, but Ehrmann could not be anyth and his treatment of life and the power that moves men an accepted as truthful.
—TER

Max Ehrmann, lecturer, dramatist, and author, has str poetical expression. Perhaps it is too soon to hail him as t poet. He is yet a young man and his work may never appea to some his lines are pure gold. His writings mark the d epoch in literature. Where others follow he has struck out self in untried paths. Nowhere does he show a trace of hav gives the world his own thoughts, spoken in his own tongue. dic, never trite; always virile, courageous and unconventi against "narrow hide-bound creeds and man-made laws," crue are but the husks of virtue, and cries out for the freedom tha onward march toward the greater good. Those who lack his are deaf to the "silent language of God's universe" will see of the whole social fabric in his teaching and will be blind t of civilization he sees.
—LEAVE

The soul of a poet and wealth of imagination.
—SAN F

Max Ehrmann is a poet of the new school—the school o false traditions and of the making of new ideals and the keepi that are strong and good.
—ST. PAUL

He stands on a high plane; and one can endure a certai tion at every convention for the sweetness of his thoughts his devotion.
—TROY

There is in his work, also, an elevation of thought, an e pose and a high, fine, moral idealism, combined with a passi

The Poems of Max Ehrmann

OTHER PUBLICATIONS BY MAX EHRMANN

BOOKS

A PRAYER AND OTHER PROSE POEMS
  Printed on Japan paper in black, gold, and colors, size 5 x 7½. Price, leatherette binding, 75 cents; ooze leather, $1.50.

WHO ENTERETH HERE AND OTHER SELECTIONS
  Decorated in color, size 5 x 7½. Price, leatherette binding, 75 cents; ooze leather, $1.50.

BREAKING HOME TIES
  A strong and helpful poem inspired by Hovenden's celebrated painting, decorated by Laura A. Humphries, size 5 x 7½. Price, cloth binding, 75 cents.

SINGLE SELECTIONS ILLUMINATED AND DECORATED

A PRAYER
  Printed on Holland parchment, size 11 x 17, hand-colored initial and gold borders. Price, 25 cents.

WHO ENTERETH HERE
  Printed in red and black upon Japanese wood with heavy cardboard mount, size 6 x 15, 50 cents; 10 x 30, $1.75.

THE HOUSE OF FORTUNE
  Motto printed on heavy Bristol board, size 9 x 11, hand-colored. Price, 50 cents.

TO YOU WHO COME AT EVENING

LOVE SOME ONE

THE GREATER HEROISM

EVENING SONG
  Leaflets in preparation.

DODGE PUBLISHING COMPANY
214-220 East 23rd Street, New York City

THE POEMS
of MAX EHRMANN

NEW YORK
DODGE PUBLISHING COMPANY
220 East 23d Street

A598635

Copyright, 1906
by Viquesney Publishing Co.

Copyright, 1910
by Dodge Publishing Co.

Contents

THE LIGHT OF THE SUN 9

PORTRAITS OF WOMEN 33
    Her Acceptance 35
    Yes or No 37
    Her Solitude 39
    Her Dream 40
    A Woman's Question 40
    The One Man 41
    I Give Myself for Love 44
    A Woman Rocking Her Child 45
    The Love-mad Huss 49
    To Her Husband 50
    He Will Come 52
    To You Who Come at Evening 53
    The Bride 54
    The One Woman 54

ON THE SHORES OF THE SKY 57
    The Awakening 59
    You with the Still Soul 60
    Who Entereth Here 61
    Letter to a Solitary 61
    I See There Is a Good Deal of Grandiloquence 63
    The Noise of the City 64
    Afield 64
    Something Will Rise in You 65
    Thou Mother 65
    O Sweet Content! 66
    Will You Come Back to Me? 66
    I Sit and Wait 67
    The Dawn 69
    One Will Pass the Door 69
    Come, You Who Are Weary 70
    On a May Morning 70
    Nothing 72
    A Child 72
    Once I Lived on a High Mountain . . . 73

The Poems of Max Ehrmann

IN THE GLOAMING AND THE NIGHT	75
The Luminous Worlds and the Love of the Night	77
Revelation	78
The Lure of the World	79
In the Night's Mysterious Stillness	80
I Go Inside and Close the Door	80
A Few Hours Ago	81
I Looked Out at the Night	81
O Lonely Workers!	82
Scorn Not the Inner Song	83
At Nightfall	84
I Go Out into the Night	84
Ere You Lie Down to Sleep	85
Good Night	85
THE BOOK OF REBELLION	87
America	89
Lamentations	89
The Greater Heroism	92
I Went into a Magnificent Church	92
I Journeyed from University to University	94
A Certain Rich Man's Dream	94
To the Masters of Men	95
Thou that Art Idle Born	96
The Enemy	97
Sunday Night	98
Desire	99
His Last Toast	99
Suicide	100
Night Meditations	101
The Fool and the City of Content	103
Myself	104
I Stood at the Crossing of Two Streets	105
I Ponder o'er Love	106
The Task	107
IN THE GARDEN OF LOVE	115
One of Long Ago	117
To Be With You	118
A Man and a Woman	119

Contents

    At the Dance 119
    While a Season Changed 120
    When I Come Home 121
    Song 122
    After the Day 123
    Let Pass 123
    The Dead Wife 124
    Love Some One 124

THE CROWDED WORLD 125
    The Crowded World 127
    The Parable of the Sea 127
    There Was a Young Artist 129
    I Know 131
    O Passer-by! 133
    You Who Wrangle with Me at the Mart . 133
    Broken Veteran of Commercial Wars . . . 134
    A Visit to a Man of Fame 135
    To-morrow 136
    The Hate and the Love of the World . . . 138
    Often in the Crowded Mart 139
    In the Hospital 139
    If You Have Made Gentler the Churlish World 140
    A Tradesman and a Poet 140
    The House of Fortune 141
    As I Returned to the Dim of My Study . . 142

TALES 145
    The Old Magnolia Tree 147
    Jeff 153

PRAYERS 163
    A Prayer 165
    An Artist's Prayer 165
    An Easter Prayer 167
    A Prayer of Summer 168
    Evening Song 168
    An Autumn Prayer 169
    Ships Returning Home 169
    Thou Whom We Call God 170

The Poems of Max Ehrmann

A Winter Prayer	170
The Last Prayer	171
CONFESSIONAL	173
Prelude	175
My Native City	175
I Sit Afraid	178
Life	178
In the Morning Twilight	179
Eheu!	181
Out of the Depths	182
Sterility	182
The Things of the Spirit	184
A Psalm	185
I Am Over Anxious	185
The House Inside	187
Through the Mist of the World	188

The Light of the Sun

PERSONS

CORONA	*blind.*
MARAH	*her companion.*
HENRY	*Marah's brother.*
MICHAL	*Corona's husband.*

THE LIGHT OF THE SUN

A balcony, enclosed at back by a balustrade. Beyond, a short distance, is the sea. The swish of the water running on the sand is heard now and then. The time is just before sunset.

CORONA enters, and feels her way along the balustrade, then across the balcony to a seat, her fingers moving nervously through the air. She is fair, tall, and of sensitive beauty.

CORONA
Marah!

MARAH
(*From within.*)
Yes, I am here, and come at once.

Enter MARAH, a dark, animated young woman. She walks to the balustrade, and looks toward the sunset and the sea.

CORONA
Marah.

MARAH
I am here by the balustrade.

CORONA
You came so softly I scarce heard your steps.

MARAH
I know how sweet the stillness is to you.

CORONA
Is Henry coming?

MARAH
I do not see him.

The Poems of Max Ehrmann

CORONA
What time is it?
MARAH
The sun begins to sink,
And all the sky is filled with crimson light.

CORONA
Within your voice there are some worship notes,
As if some one you loved had pressed your lips.

MARAH
It is the wonder of the western sky
That makes one ache for whispered words at dusk,
For tenderness that drives away all care,
As dark pursues the lingering light of day.

CORONA
Do you see all of this within the sky?

MARAH
Corona, often have I wondered why
It is the evening that we women love.

CORONA
Because it is the time of coming home,
When they afield and journeying seek for rest.
Oh! often have I tried, but all in vain,
To see again the sky I must have seen
Ere darkness closed its door and shut me in.
But almost nothing I remember now
Except my mother's face. (*Calling.*) Marah!

MARAH
I listen.

The Light of the Sun

CORONA

And I have told you how it comes to me
At night as I lie still and wait for sleep.
I think in all the world there must be naught
As wonderful as my sweet mother's face.
O Marah, tell me of the western sky.
I understand you better than the others.
Did you not say it was like tenderness?

MARAH

Like tenderness.

CORONA

          Then all things beautiful
Out there bring tenderness. I understand.

MARAH

Yes.

CORONA

Then is Michal unto me the god
Of beauty. When I hear his distant voice,
As he comes up the way, I tremble here,
(*Placing her hand on her breast.*)
And drink the sound as one all day athirst.
His touch of hand is sunset unto me,
His lips make me forget my eyes are dim.
O Marah!—are you listening?

MARAH

          Yes, I listen.

The Poems of Max Ehrmann

CORONA

The sunset is no lure to me, nor moon,
Nor stars, nor dawn; of these you often speak,
And often I have heard since childhood years.
But him would I behold who sent the rain
Upon my leaves, and made the birds to sing
Upon each branch within my lightless woods.
Do you remember how I used to sit
Disconsolate, like brooding winter time,
Or like some agéd woman by a fire
Who freezing waits the kindly touch of death?
When Michal came and softly pressed my lips,
I who was never born began to live
And feel in me the breath of things unknown.

MARAH

(*Smiling.*)
Quite eloquent you grow.

CORONA

     Were you not so
A moment since? I feel you're smiling now.
I tell you, Marah, life is naught to me
Excepting as I live in this great love;
And death's cold kiss were sweet when it is gone.

The Light of the Sun

MARAH
(*Coming to her.*)
Dear heart, 'tis true I did a moment smile.
But what if you and I were both deceived,
My wondrous sunset but an empty thing
That lives within my wandering mind alone,
Your kingly Michal but a restless dream
That agitates a cavern of your brain!
O'er all of us illusion spreads her wings
Like birds that warmly nurse their brood at dusk.
The things that now you crave to see may take
Away your joy.

CORONA
      Your speech is strange to-night.
I like it not, and understand it not.
Dear Marah, often now it seems to me
You plunge your mind in these chill waves of thought.
I will not follow you, the world is sweet
And warm. Look out and see if Henry comes.

MARAH
I look, but do not see him on the way.

CORONA
Does tenderness still glow within the west?

MARAH
More beautiful it grows.

The Poems of Max Ehrmann

CORONA
          Come, play a while;
Too serious we have been. Do tell me, Marah,
Is your nose as straight and thin as mine, thus.
(*Stroking her nose.*)

MARAH
(*Laughing.*)
I'm glad 'tis much like yours.

CORONA
              But Michal's curves.
And here (*indicating*) just here doth have a little hump.
Is it somewhat the same with other men?

MARAH
'Tis much the same with them.

CORONA
            Who's coming now?

MARAH
I hear no steps.

CORONA
    'Tis Henry, I am sure.

MARAH
(*Looking out by the balustrade.*)
'Tis he.

CORONA
    I would that he did hurry now,
For he will bring me words of joy, I know.

The Light of the Sun

MARAH
What words?

CORONA
        O Marah! you shall hear at once.
I feel that ere the light of day is past
I shall behold the world I crave to see,
And your dear sunset, but o'er all his face!
Long have I nursed this hope till now it lives;
And Henry, too, has bent his will to this,
That I shall see, and walk no more in darkness.
I have not told you, for you had no faith
That I should ever look upon the world.
(*Rising.*)
O Henry, Henry, speed your steps to me,
Who knock and wait before the door of light!
        Enter HENRY.

HENRY
Good news! To-morrow he will come whose art
Will send the sunlight bounding through your eyes.
He bade me counsel you prepare to see,
For very near at hand may be the hour
When you will look upon the sunlit world.
'Tis said the fault lies not within your eyes,
For they are like twin stars set in the night;
And soon—oh, very soon may be the time
When wide the doors will swing to let light in!
Corona, now—perhaps this very hour
You'll cast aside the leaden cloak of night!
Oh, then we four shall dance upon the air,
And make such revels as befits our joy!
There's no mistake, I do report aright!

The Poems of Max Ehrmann

MARAH

Henry—

CORONA

(*Feeling her way to* HENRY. *Interrupting.*)
      Nay, Marah, you must let me speak.
I swear to God if He will give me light,
That I may once behold my human god,
I'll be as bending as a babe in arms
Unto His will, and ne'er complain again
No matter what the slight of nature be!
How often in the evening have I sat
With Michal by my side, and heard his voice,
That stilled the tumult of my restless soul,
My truant hand would steal into his own—
Oh! I have felt inside my head, it seemed
Just back of both my eyes, an urging force
Within the nerves that strove to break the wall,
Like some wild beast that beats the iron bars.
And now this urging force begins again,
I feel the throbs each time it strikes a blow.
Already I do know that light is born
Within the darkened chamber of my brain;
Already I do look upon the world—
Our world—his world and mine! The sunlit sea
Shall woo me, too, and so the wandering moon;
And I with mine own eyes shall him behold
Who raised me from the dead and taught me life.
Where is he, Henry? I must find him now.
(*She feels her way out, calling.*)
O Michal, Michal!

The Light of the Sun

MARAH

        See what you have wrought!
Her brain have you set going as the wind;
Her hope is sharpened like an edgéd shaft
That will but cruelly pierce her to the quick,
If failure doom this doubtful enterprise.

HENRY

It will not fail. I'm sure it will not fail.

MARAH

A thousand times more mischief have you wrought!
Oh! you yourself are blinder than the blind,
Your eyes are open, yet you cannot see!
The trees you see, the sunset, and the moon;
But wandering moons and sunsets made of dreams,
That lift our lowly life to higher heights,
Have never set their torch within your brain.
Think—do we live by sight and sound alone?
Far more we dwell within the gilded house
That fancy garnishes with beaten gold.

HENRY

I do not understand. What harm if light
Be brought to her to look upon the world?
I did but think to do a kindly deed.
You love Corona dearly—do you not?

MARAH

A thousand times I love her more than you,
For I would leave her to her world of dreams,
Far sweeter than this world that we both see.

The Poems of Max Ehrmann

She wanders in a garden where each flower,
Though it lack form and hue, is spirit made;
Her heart is tenderer than springtime dawn.
Has she not taught us all that life is good?
'Tis so because her world herself she makes.
What she would think as true, is true for her;
Because she cannot with her eyes disprove.
While we with eyes live but a moment's bliss,
When we in daydreams run away and leave
Our eyes behind. Oh! can't you understand?

HENRY
I own I do not understand your meaning
That blindness better is than sight.

MARAH
                                    O Henry,
Must I spell out the words, pronounce each letter?

HENRY
You are unlike yourself. I'll hear no more.

MARAH
Wait, for we both stand this quiet evening
Before the door of a disrupted house.
Often have I been seized with fear that light
Might one day burst into her sightless eyes,
And she too suddenly behold the world.
Her eyes are clear and look like mine and yours,
Save they are dreamier than distant stars
Upon a summer night. Now mark my words:
Long have I known by simple touch of skill,
Or by some chance, or by the growth of time,
That sunlight through Corona's eyes might course,
But silent have I kept.

The Light of the Sun

HENRY

Oh, monstrous!

MARAH

And Michal, too, has known.

HENRY

More monstrous!

MARAH

And fearful have we been that she might see.

HENRY

What touch of hell has tainted both your souls!
Contamination has been brooding here,
And you would blind me with your sophistry!

MARAH

Yourself shall punish you for speech like this.

HENRY

I'll hear no more.

MARAH

You shall hear all at once.
Though pained, I pass the sting you gave just now.

HENRY

What more is there to hear than I have heard!
With your own lips have you condemned yourself.

The Poems of Max Ehrmann

MARAH

Be careful else you burn the only bridge
That lies between us two. You shall hear more.
I'll spell the words. Oh! with your noble face
How can you be as stupid as a child!
We two shall sadly part some day in death,
I beg, therefore, you listen to my words.
Corona wanders in a joyous world
That is not ours, a world of beauty made;
And if that world be marred, it is her death.
Her love for Michal is— Oh, you, a man,
How can you understand a woman's love!
A thousand, thousand times more dear that love
Than your desire for my own chastity.
He is the balmy summer air she breathes,
Her consolation by the winter fire;
And in the night she sleeps within his arms;
And once she told me that he wakened her
With kisses on her lips each breaking morn.
And you, O brother, you would this destroy!
For think of him the Michal of her dreams,
And him the Michal that we daily see;
(MICHAL *has entered at back, and stands unobserved.*
  His face is terrible to behold.)
The ugly pot the potter marred in making,
The face bedaubed with scarlet marks from birth.
Oh! often have I looked upon his face,
And gone without and spat to purge myself;
As if the goodly air we both did breathe
Were poisoned by his breath. If he by chance
Did touch me with his lips, some lapse in nature
Would my flesh derange with torturing pain,
Like women who are slighted in their birth.

The Light of the Sun

His eyes are like the eyes I've seen in swine,
Blinking from out their pulpy bed of mire.
Corona feels his strong and gentle soul;
And he within the gallery of her mind
Is like some noble-featured, happy prince,
On whom the gods have done their choicest work.
O you, my brother, will not rend her world,
And place a leech upon her tender throat!
We all do wander in our different dreams;
Let her abide in hers, her love of him.
(*Turning, she sees* MICHAL.)
Ugh! Look, Henry!

HENRY
Michal, have you o'erheard?

MICHAL
I have o'erheard, but I am dead within,
And blame her not. We both have lived a lie.
O Marah! I would come and take your hand,
But I would spare your eyes and touch the pain;
I was not made for daytime, but the night,
And have no heart to look upon myself.
My mother oft did tell me long ago
That I a suckling babe did pain her breast;
And while I pressed for drink, her eyes she closed.
In childhood human playmates had I none.
The dogs were kinder, for I stroked their fur;
And all my early love I gave to them,
For they alone were pleased to be by me.
And as the world its back upon me turned,
Not harder but more tender grew my heart.
I dared not go about in time of day,
Lest by some jeer my soul be made to bleed.

The Poems of Max Ehrmann

The night had all affection for my youth;
I lay upon its bosom like a child,
And loved the candled starlight of the sky.
I trod the silver of the milky ways,
As one would journey in his native land;
And worshiped as an ardent neophyte
Bows low in prayer before his soul's own god.
Each star did speak to me in silent speech
The language of the cities made of gold.
The soft night wind did fill my listening ears
With music strange from out some distant world;
And all the sorrow of the ages past
Was sweet to me, for I was made of sorrow.
The mighty pillars deep within my soul
Were laid there by my sorrow, calm and strong;
And I had learned of sorrow how to love,
And sorrow drove me forth into the night
Where I might freely look upon the world.
And often in the night I walked abroad,
And spoke with men who could not see my face.
And women at the nightly festivals
Oft wandered from the crowd to quiet lanes;
And there, enshrouded by the kindly dark,
My boyish lips did speak with them.
And once Corona came. With her alone
I dared to walk beneath the sun and moon.
And then we both did meet again, again,
Until none dared to part us, for like mine
Her life was bound forever in this love.
At first when I did speak of lacking grace
Of feature, I was bidden to be silent;
She said I was but weary and disheartened,
Denying me the right to judge myself.

The Light of the Sun

When oft again I spoke, she would not hear,
And playful, like a child, did stop her ears.
The tide of love did bear us quickly hence;
It seemed as if the gods did guide our course.
Together grew the fiber of our lives,
Ere I could think what had befallen us.
To her I wear the visage of a king.
Oh! I have wronged Corona, and should die!

MARAH

I, too, have wronged her.

HENRY

                        I much more than both.

MICHAL

My soul is sick as one who looks on death.

MARAH

O Michal! grieve no more, let tears be mine,
If I could weep, at once I'd call them forth.
We all do love her as a mother loves,
Save you, who worship—
(CORONA *heard calling near the balustrade.*)
                        Michal! Michal!

MARAH

                                Peace!
Now let our wills be masters of ourselves.
Let not this house of glass break at our feet.
(CORONA *nearer.*)
O Michal! Michal!

The Poems of Max Ehrmann

MICHAL
I shall speak to her.

MARAH
It must not be, we are distracted yet,
And should betray ourselves. Let her pass on,
Till we in calm bethink what shall be done.
For love of her forbear, forbear to speak!
Break not the golden dream. Let her pass on.
(*Whispering.*)
Now silence.
(*A pause.*)
CORONA *enters.*

CORONA
(*Feeling her way along the balustrade.*)
    Michal, Michal!
(*Farther on.*)   Michal! Michal!
(*Near the end of the balustrade.*)
O Marah, Henry, Michal, Michal! Gone.
(*Lifting her arms toward* MICHAL. *Joyfully.*)
O Michal, Michal! I shall see you, Michal!
(CORONA *passes off. Heard in the distance.*)
Michal, Michal!
(*A pause. More faintly.*)
    Michal, Michal!

MARAH
      Quickly,
My brother, follow close behind her steps,
So nothing that is ill befall her now.
She wanders in a maddened fit of joy.
        (*Exit* HENRY.)

The Light of the Sun

MICHAL
With her enshrouded eyes she stared at me,
And I beheld the hate of all the world.
The stars of all my life dash through the sky.
The end is near. If she behold my face,
I am as one already mute in death.

MARAH
Speak not too loud lest we be overheard.
Although I cannot look upon your face,
I see your soul, and inwardly I weep.
A thousand, thousand lies I've lived for you;
Because your heart is tender as a rose,
And you her lonely life have filled with love.
I'll serve you to the limit of my power.
Now let us both arouse our saner selves,
And think what shall be done. Come, come, Michal,
And draw thyself together, like the soul
I know thou art.

MICHAL
    Already she is changed,
The light is piercing through her starless night.

MARAH
Come, come, this is the image made of fear.
I'll go myself and cool her flaming mind,
That withers up the garden of her life.
Stay here till I return; and then we three
Shall try our might to smother out her hope.

MICHAL
I cannot, she hath set her soul on this.

The Poems of Max Ehrmann

MARAH
Forbear to speak to her till I return.
If power be mine this temple shall not fall.
(*Starts off as* HENRY *enters.*)

HENRY
Marah, she still calls for you and Michal,
And laughs and weeps as does a fitful child;
She bade me quickly find and fetch her husband.
"Ah, first of all my eyes shall drink him in,"
She says again and o'er again, and thus
And thus she smites her forehead with her hand.
What shall be done?

MICHAL
    I'll go to her at once,
While yet her eyes are without earthly light.
She suffers now, I cannot stay. (*Starts off.*)

HENRY
      Michal,
Wait, look!

MARAH
    She comes and does not feel her way.
Be silent both and let me speak to her.
(*A pause.*)
(CORONA *heard calling in the distance.*)
Michal, Michal!
(*Nearer.*)
    Michal, Michal!
(*She enters.*)

The Light of the Sun

CORONA

(*Agitated.*) Marah!

MARAH

Corona, do a moment calm yourself.

CORONA

O touch me not!

MARAH

I am not touching you.

CORONA

Yes, yes you are; your hand is on my head.
A piercing pain runs through my throat and breast.
(*Moving frantically backward and foward.*)
Michal, Michal! Tell me, where is he? Speak!
This instant something comes to life in me.
O Marah, something batters at my head,
It is the world outside that would come in,
And light the candles of my darkened house!

MARAH

Corona!—

CORONA

Nay, let me enjoy this birth,
For to myself I now bring forth a world,
The world you oft have told me of—tenderness,
The world of him I love.
(*Abruptly facing the sunset. A piercing cry.*)
Look, look, the sun!

The Poems of Max Ehrmann

Michal, Marah, the world is born—I see!
(*Throws herself about* HENRY'S *neck.*)
Michal, Michal! (*Pressing her face against his.*)
                Michal, Michal, kiss me!
Thou heaven born, why art thou silent now?
My eyes do drink thee in. My lips do thirst.
Oh, moisten thou my lips with seas of love!
O Michal, speak, that I may hear thy voice
And see thee all at once—Michal, Michal!
Draw not away from me, loose not my grasp;
Thy touch is cold, and palsied is thy tongue!

HENRY

Let me but stand aside.

CORONA

              Thy voice—thy voice!
(*Drawing away.*)
'Tis changed—'tis not thy voice—'tis Henry's voice!
Michal, Michal, where is he—where is he?
(*Faces* MICHAL, *shrinking.*)
Who is this?

MARAH

(*Quickly.*)   A stranger just come to us.

CORONA

(*To* MICHAL.)
Begone, thy face doth hurt my new-born sight.

MARAH

He came to tell us Michal—

The Light of the Sun

CORONA

(*Interrupting.*) Let him speak.

MARAH

(*Quickly*)
He cannot, he is mute.

CORONA

You said he came
To tell—

MARAH

(*Interrupting.*)
He did but motion with his hands.

CORONA

Take him away, I will not look on him,
His face doth sicken me.
(MICHAL *drawing a dagger stabs himself in the breast.*)

MARAH

(*Rushing toward him.*)
Michal! Michal!
Great God, forbear—forbear! Michal! Michal!

CORONA

Give me the dagger, I will pierce my eyes,
And sit again with Michal in the night.

The Poems of Max Ehrmann

HENRY
(*Seizing her.*)
Corona—

CORONA
   I grow sick, my limbs grow weak;
Some fit of dreaming has turned cold my blood.
The hand—the withered hand that holds the knife—
Oh! wake me, Michal! Michal! (*Sinking on his body.*)
                Michal! Michal!

CURTAIN

Portraits of Women

HER ACCEPTANCE

I'LL give my answer now, dear; it is "yes."
More gently or you'll hurt me—yet 'tis bliss—
Now but once more, and—and once more—'tis bliss!
Wait, dear; let us sit still a while and talk,
You in that chair and I in this one here,
A little while, not long, I'm sure you will.
I wish to tell you something—now, to-night,
Before we go too far in this new way.
You do not start; that shows your faith in me:
It is about my future, not my past,
You know I have not lived much in my life;
But I have thought and seen the lives of others,
Of women who have gone with men in marriage.
Don't be impatient, dear, I'll not be long;
I know you think it is some idle tale
By which I hope to make you laugh—but no.
And please—a little while; I cannot think,
I only dream, when you have hold my hand.
So—that is better, you off there, I here—
A little while.
             I have but one regret,
I wish I came to you as free as air.
A few of us can come to men that way,
By fortune favored with inheritance,
Or by some genius, got I know not how.
But most of us come sadly empty handed.
The world will not let us come otherwise,
And we are still dependent creatures all.
I wish you did not have to buy me, dear.
I am so much degraded by the sale
That were you some one else I should not sell.

The Poems of Max Ehrmann

O that I were as free to choose as you,
And yet I'm sure I should choose only you.
When once I go from here to be with you,
I'll be a heavy weight upon your back.
Alone you might have freely gone your way,
No common slave of endless dreary toil;
But now you bind yourself upon the rocks
For me and little children born of us.
And should you fail of cunning at your task,
And fail to work and lie and bind men down
To serve your aim for gold, then all is done
With you; then must you sweat until you die.
Because of me you'll grind and sweat the more;
And unborn babes will cry into your ears
With voices real that whip your tired life
To longer hours. And your sad drudgery
I cannot help; 'twill pierce me to the soul.
And though I suffer, too, and daily toil,
Eternal servant of a child's caprice,
I still shall be a weight upon your back.

Ah! now your heart is filled with noble things,
Love, music, and the sky. You walk on clouds,
The world is as a garden set with jewels,
And softly sweetened as a room perfumed.
For you all this shall change as I have said,
I hear you groan beneath your heavy load,
I feel no more your tender, sweet young soul,
I see your head bound down upon your task,
Lest some one steal your task and take our bread.
At this great cost you pay for me, and I—
I should deny you nothing at this price.
And through the ages women somehow know,

Portraits of Women

By history taught, that they must yield themselves.
This is the thing they give for the price men pay,
Although it often be a gift of shame.
And I have known some in this commerce long,
Returning every piece of gold they cost
With outraged inches of their tender flesh.
Dear heart, with us let it be otherwise;
And though you pay for me this bitter price,
Still let us both be owners of ourselves,
And never touch save out of love.—Kiss me.

YES OR NO

(Suggested by the painting of Sir John Millais.)

I KNOW my heart and yet I answer not,
For some I've seen grow sad by deep regret.
Better than love that fails is solitude,
Barren and hungry-hearted to the last.
It has still the happiness of day dreams,
For love that fails awakes the sleeper quick
With ruthless hands of saddened memory.
Better is solitude that still is sweet
In thought and not unkindly looked upon,
Whose virgin cheeks remember not love's kiss
At break of dawn nor in night's deepest sleep,
Whose breast is strange to touch of children's lips.
Far better not to know love's throbbing joy,
Than sadly to remember love is dead,
And hear cold words that once were soft and sweet,
And feel no more the press of eager arms
Where oft thy head did lie in bliss at eve,
And deign to beg where once thou didst permit.
Give me stern love that's fierce in jealousy,

The Poems of Max Ehrmann

Ardent, like love that's born by open fields
In silence save the soft winds whispering,
And grows each starry night by garden stile,
And lingers late before the last farewell;
So strange and wondrous sweet it would not part
But for the swiftly moving pallid stars
That call ere long the noiseless break of dawn;
Love that does not forget the first sweet kiss,
The gentle, hesitating touch of hand,
That blissful calm that made us one at first
By cheerful glow of winter evening fire;
Such love that stronger grows through changing years,
When age shall steal the rose from off my cheek
And dim my eyes and bend me slowly down.
And in that distant time wilt thou forget
The ancient trees 'neath which we sat at dusk,
And how, like twilight's spreading dark, our souls
Went forth with night's still music o'er the world,
And we both dwelt again in olden times
By glistening shores of sun-kissed golden seas,
And heard the echoed songs of all the world
Resound as softer grew the thickening dark?
Love's music old, wilt thou then break the reed
In twain by cruel neglect of thy warm lips?
Or wilt thou find the music sweeter still,
Like early childhood's oft-repeated songs?
Though I pale before thee on life's long way,
Wilt thou then still find joy in all my smiles?
And sit with gladness by my side at eve?
And walk with me through memory's olden lanes,
To mark again the hallowed spots where first
Thou kissed my cheek and shyly spoke my name—
Where once with saddened hearts we quarreled a while,

Portraits of Women

And thou with moistened eyes besought my love,
Which was again thine own ere thou didst ask—
And where in shade of yonder sighing woods
Oft tranced I sat and listened to thy hopes,
And silently implored a part in all
Close by thy side through joyous coming years?
When once I give thee all wilt thou forget,
In stress of other things, to kiss the lips
That yearn for thee by lonely evening light?
Then wilt thou whisper in my ear as now,
And set astir the chords of love's sweet dream,
And say the things that draw me close to thee
Ere slumber close our eyes in still of night?
I hear again thy oft repeated vows.
Would thou wert nigh to still my wavering thoughts,
And speak once more the words that are my bliss—
That feed my heart which thou hast hunger taught.

HER SOLITUDE

MY LIFE is still to-night, no bitterness,
Nor joy; and but one endless thought creeps out,
As dreaming here I sit and think about
My days that pass without dear love's caress.
And yet, O God! I cannot, cannot guess
Why lonely I must dwell and ever doubt
The time will come when he, my own, will rout
My fears and all my restless heart's distress.
Why didst thou plant in me this longing so
That in my wake and sleep forever calls
And yet beyond my pale of fortune falls?
Not always I'll be young, the bloom will go.
All this, O God! I have not understood.
Am I not worthy—have not I been good?

The Poems of Max Ehrmann

HER DREAM

I THOUGHT I lived with you beneath a sun
Whose golden rays ne'er left the deep blue sky,
But shone and shone where rolling meadows lie
With dew as when the day had just begun,
And danced in leafy vales where waters run
And where the sweet brook's murmurs never die,
And on the mountain peak's so still and high
Which all but fearless strong-winged birds must shun.
I thought that time went sweet and soft and slow,
And left no marks save those of gentleness
That bound you to my life with strong caress;
And you saw naught but all my soul's deep truth,
No fading bloom, nor form the years bent low,
But ever still the beauty of my youth.

A WOMAN'S QUESTION

AM I not meek?
I give my hand, my lips, my cheek,
My dear, to you,
My life, my soul; and shall not rue.

Sink deep in joy
And revel long; I'll be your toy,
My dear. From now
To play the part you'll teach me how.

To your desire
Of dawn and dark, though like the fire,
My dear, I yield,
As withered grass in a burning field.

Portraits *of* Women

> Your heart's caprice,
> For all of me, will it ne'er cease,
> My dear, to cling
> To both the flesh and soul I bring?

THE ONE MAN

THE written law and the custom had denied me love. But as with other women, instinct had taught me to be silent. I was in the flower of my youth, and each day I hungered more and more.

Still, when I uttered a sound, the elders raised their fingers, and shamed me to silence, saying that love was only according to the written law and the custom.

Thus a year passed, and several years passed, and the flower of my youth began to fade, and the eternal hunger in my heart made me sick of soul, and joy was no more in me.

Then one night I lifted my eyes again to the god of my childhood, and again earnestly I sought an answer in the stars; when lo! I saw that the written law and the custom were man-made, and that the hunger in my heart and the flower of my youth were God-made.

And I trod forth in the middle of the night to yield myself to the arms that would hold me fast, and to the lips that would moisten mine. And my heart beat as never before, and the stars sang, and the night and the god of the night smiled upon me.

The Poems of Max Ehrmann

And when I came to the arms that would hold me fast and the lips that would moisten mine to give myself up, I said, "Here, pluck the flower of my youth, and feed my heart."

But the arms of him I loved were listless and would entwine me not, nor would his lips press mine; and there was some talk, and I cried aloud bitterly, understanding not. Then said he I loved, "The written law and the custom would crucify you on the street before all the people."

I went away, and walked in the dim night, wondering why the people should deny the will of God, and punish them that obey His command, for the love in me was heaven-born.

And soon thereafter I returned to him I loved, and said, "I will endure the punishment of the written law and the custom, touch me, touch me, touch me with your hand! and I will proclaim my joy aloud; for what is wrought in love's name is justified of God."

"Then," said he, "must you perish, for they that need the written law and the custom will not hold them guiltless that need it not."

"Death be welcome," I cried, "better a thousand times to live an hour and love and die at once, in the night, or be stoned upon the street, than die by inches, to wither and rot, and grow into old age as some unwatered flowerless vine, creeping over the juiceless earth, ugly to behold and barren."

Portraits *of* Women

"Wait," palliated my love, "perhaps all shall be fulfilled even yet according to the written law and the custom. Wait!"

"Waited have I all these years. The fruit is ripe, the time is here, it is the season. See, I am still beautiful, the rose still lights my cheek, my eyes not yet are dim, my bosom breathes like wind-swept fields of grain, and I nightly dream the dream of women loved!"

Then he said, "The written law and the custom are for the good of all the people, and the good of all the people is the will of God. Wait!"

"No," I cried, "I will have my hand touched by you whom I love. I will walk with you in the evening and in the night unafraid, and I will not part from you; the dawn shall be a knell for twain in your house, and the dusk shall not divide us."

"Wait!" said he again.

"I will tear down the walls that surround me, break the locks that imprison me, pull back the veil that blinds me. A mountain of laws shall not deny me, nor a sea of ice freeze my desire. I was made to breathe the sweet, and though death steal upon me at dusk, this day shall I follow the voice of the stars and the god of the stars."

Softly he said, "Too much I love you;" and touching me with his hand, he led me to where the day was darkening; and long we sat and spake no word, for the tumult was not of human speech; and soon the night came, and the stars crept through the dark; yet spake he no word, nor touched me again with his hand.

And after a long time, in perfect calm, he whispered, "We will obey the law;" and arising, we wandered slowly off together, out into the light and the world.

I GIVE MYSELF FOR LOVE

O YOU who love me, do you wish to bind
   Me fast; when you grow cold
That no escape I find?

My heart I cannot barter for all days,
Though swearing with my tongue
A thousand, thousand ways.

The house of love is spirit, and no key
Will firmly close its doors
Forever and for thee.

Yet if you love but me, the one true way,
Without agreements long,
I'll go with you to-day.

But if by spring or noon of summer you
Look sad upon my face,
We'll smile and say adieu.

Glad, glad that we have tasted to the core
The sweet of all the world,
Though we shall taste no more.

Portraits of Women

For this I give my all—below, above,
On earth, and after it—
I give myself for love.

A WOMAN ROCKING HER CHILD

"I SEE that you are rocking him again."
"Oh, yes!"

"You're spoiling him by custom of that sort,
And, too, you tire yourself, who need more rest."

'I love to rock him so each night."

'Shall I recount to you a gruesome tale?"

'Yes, if you like."

'Then stop, don't rock a while."

'No, no, it might awaken him. See how
He sleeps. I listen now; recite the tale
By which for sport you seek to frighten me.
I'm not afraid, too rich am I in joy."

"It is the history of a child, like him.
To make the tale more real, it *is* the child
You rock so softly now as he shall live
Till death has gently kissed you on the lips.
For months his mother, *you,* will toil for him
From morn's first twilight till the day is done.
And though you're worn, you'll rock him every evening.
Soon one by one the breaths of each disease
Will seek to quench the candle of his life,

Until his tender flesh shall livid grow;
And every time 'twill be like letting blood
Directly from the chambers of your heart.
Then you, on his account, stabbed at his birth,
And worn by days of anxious servitude,
Shall fall so deep into the gaping pit
Of death that life will seem far off and strange.
If this you knew would surely come to pass
Would you as now continue rocking him?"

"Oh, yes!"

"A lusty child in his eleventh year—
One day while chastening him, he'll strike you back;
And there will be a bruise upon your hip.
Would you continue rocking him—?"

"Yes, yes!"

"Until his fifteenth year a million times
He will annoy you with his many wants;
And you shall be this wanton's perfect victim.
One day, with friends, some worthless thing he'll steal;
And you will humbly go before the judge
And plead for him, inside the prisoners' dock.
This shame will be a poison in your blood.
Will you continue rocking him?"

"Yes."

"He will be handsome—"

"Oh, I am sure of that!"

Portraits of Women

"He will be handsome, and at twenty-four
A maid he'll wed against her father's wish.
Though rich, he'll turn the lovers from his door.
And you will plan, economize, and toil
For years, as one in bondage held by them,
That these two idle ones shall feel no want.
Knowing that, will you continue rocking him?"

"Yes."

"Then some years more, when you are stooped with care,
Her father, reconciled, will bid them come
And live with him; and they will be installed
Behind the battlements of all his wealth.
Will you be happy then?"

"Yes, yes!"

"The years are moving swiftly; there will be
Some white and silver hair upon your head,
And forward you will stoop a little more,
And your right limb will pain you with each step.
You will not often get to see your son.
One day henceforth he will avoid your calls;
And you'll be asked to come in at the rear,
The servants' entrance. You will sway a little,
As one who's hurt, and part of you will die.
That true, will you continue rocking him,
Who lies so helpless there within your arms?"

"Yes."

"That other sweeter tie is snapped by death,
And you will be alone in all the world—

The Poems of Max Ehrmann

Alone, except this full-grown man, your son.
One day his wife, whom you had spared from want,
Will tell you not to kiss her children's lips,
Because—you will not hear the reason given;
And you will speak of it to him, your son;
And he will tell you that he has no time
To listen to the twaddle of old age;
And he will go to join his jolly friends,
And you will sit alone. If you knew that
Would you continue rocking him?"

"Yes."

"Then there will be a mighty scene take place;
The actors will be he, his wife, and you.
Your head will be the color of the snow,
And there will be a tremor in your voice,
Your eyes will be moist with the sorrows of age.
You'll speak to him of recent ills you bore,
Injustices provoked by him and her;
You will recount the love of other years,
His childhood, how you rocked him in the dark,
And nursed him year by year with tender care.
But he will shake his head impatiently,
And speak as if he had not heard your words.
Henceforth your every action will be watched,
As one that wanders in uncertain dreams;
And gone will be the world you knew in youth,
And loneliness will sit within your soul.
Will you continue rocking him?"

"Yes."

"And then at last you'll gladly fall asleep;
And as you go out to your earthen bed,

Portraits of Women

He'll have his empty carriage follow you.
Would you indeed continue rocking him
If this—all this—you knew would come to pass?"

"Yes."

"I cannot understand."

"Of course you can't."

"Again I say I cannot understand."

"Of course you can't, you're but his father, dear."

THE LOVE-MAD HUSS'

AT EVE hard by Neponset's crystal wave—
　　Neponset's gleaming wave—
I saw her last. The night was wild,
The dark fell fast, and cold the blast,
　And all alone she ran;
Along the snowy path no sound she gave
That eve hard by Neponset's crystal wave.

Her pallid face, part hid by fallen hair,
　Long, streaming, waving hair,
The wind made rise and fall and curl;
And wild the guise about her eyes
　As she ran by me swift,
All open at the throat, her arms both bare,
Her pallid face part hid by fallen hair.

The Poems of Max Ehrmann

I watched her as she sped along the night,
  The glimmer of the night,
Till she was gone. I went to rest,
Yet ever on until the dawn
  She ran within my sleep,
Her hair awry, her face a haggard white—
I watched her as she sped along the night.

Next morning as I walked upon the shore,
  Neponset's blustrous shore,
I saw barred tight a mourning house,
To mark the flight a soul that night
  Had made. Of one I asked,
"Who's dead?"—"The love-mad huss, she is no more—
Was found at dawn upon the frozen shore."

Now ever on that gusty, fitful shore,
  Neponset's icy shore,
I see her go through night's wild blast,
In lonely woe, still to and fro;
  The marble face, the eyes
Of withered white—she paces evermore
Upon Neponset's fitful, icy shore.

TO HER HUSBAND

I THOUGHT of our wedding, a long time ago,
  The noise that it made and the grand public show.
You said I was charmingly beautiful, dear—
You're thinking it still? That sounds good to the ear
Of even a wife who is losing no sleep
Concerning the love that she never could keep.
I knew you were rich, but you're much richer now.
How mad we both were on our hearing of how

Portraits of Women

The friend of our bosom depicted us two
As animal things with ideas so few!
When once you've extracted his joy-giving juice—
A friend—what's a friend but a thing for abuse?
If life never taught us another dread thing,
It taught us that lesson with many a sting.
It seems long ago that we lived through that day.
I'm weary again and without much delay
Should leave you at once for a journey quite far—
You say you'd be glad if I went to a star?
It's pitiful how we both sit here and stare,
All wilted inside in this stifling air.
Each time I came back from my journeying, then
We lighted the candle of pleasure again.
It burned and it burned and it much smaller grew,
And every time it went out for us two.
I'm fearing to go and return through that door,
The candle is spent and will burn nevermore.
And you've gone away several times in the past,
And when you returned did the thing ever last?
How clever we've been in our conduct—and why?
You're never annoyed with a wee baby's cry,
You're never annoyed with a few weeks of scare
That I shall be bringing a boisterous heir.
How cunning I am! You should like me for that,
I've never been careless and ugly and fat.
You show me with pride, and I oft play the part
A woman who's clever can play well by heart.
But that is outside; it is different here.
You've always been good; I don't loathe you, my dear.
I thought of the words that the minister used
That night when he called and so much us amused;
And yet of his cant I've been thinking a lot.

The Poems of Max Ehrmann

I laughed at the time, but I've not quite forgot.
His words ran like this, I've been saying them o'er,
"In things of the flesh you should barter no more;
Not even by law is such barter made right:
I fear you are bodies, not souls, in God's sight."
That sounds, does it not, as if we were both lost?
You never complained of the price that I cost.
I've paid in return—have I not, my dear sir?—
I'm going to bed; but now please don't infer
I hate you a bit, for I don't. Like a ball
Our lives keep on rolling and rolling, that's all.

HE WILL COME

HE WILL come, she said
  Deep in her bounding, girlish heart, and smiled,
   Assurance on her lips;
And childhood's dreaming fancies wild
   That over blissful pathways led—
He will come, she said.

  He will come, she said,
As many daily tasks and years came on;
   And from her cherry lips
And cheeks the girlish glow had gone;
   And though her glad, wild dreams had fled—
He will come, she said.

  He will come, she said,
As o'er the saddened chords of her pure heart
   The hand of bitterness
Oft now and then a tune would start,
   When some old playmate's life was wed—
He will come, she said.

Portraits of Women

  He will come, she said,
And sweetly smiled with faith again serene
  In that one perfect love
Beyond the faded and the green
  Of earth. Ere last they laid her dead,
He has come, she said.

TO YOU WHO COME AT EVENING

I KNOW you oft have told me, dear,
The world is full of hate and strife;
But I'm content with you and life—
With you each night beside me here.

You often fear that I am sad,
Because some things you think I miss;
I would not lose a single kiss
For that which makes some persons glad.

And when you touch me with your hand,
And say the words you used to say,
Why—all the night is turned to day,
And I forget the things I'd planned.

And often when we here have sat,
And I have said, "Tell me again,"
I've seen you smile a bit, but then,
You see, we women live on that.

We women love that we may live;
The heart is hungry, too, and I—
No matter if you don't know why—
Well, I'm content with what you give.

The Poems of Max Ehrmann

THE BRIDE

YOU tremble, dear. See, I am not afraid,
And all myself I give; my heart is light;
The crimson on my cheek should flee in fright,
And yet does not; 'tis there delayed
Because I have no fear. I oft have prayed,
With warming breath of whispers in the night,
For this sweet hour with you, and tight
Have clasped my hands, as in my thoughts you strayed.
My lips I've saved for you and all the cheer
That summer's dewy morns tossed in my heart,
That when at eve you're wearied, I might start
Some trifling little talk, which all the fear
Of morrows and the day should swiftly part
From you, and make you glad that I am here.

THE ONE WOMAN

HOW could I help but love you, coming up a cool and radiant fountain in the hot and dreary night of life?
I swear the sins of youthful women lay upon my hands, the grimy sweat of wearied men in strife,
Who'd clothed my body with garments fair, and the agonies of children, too, condemned to toil that I might freely live.
I swear the cries of beaten slaves turned not my ear, nor wails of stunted children that the sea of want doth give.
There was no order in my days. I slept and ate as instinct called, and heeded every wanton passion near,
A face, a form, a game of chance, the gossip of the idle wags, and lived to finish quickly earth's career.

Portraits of Women

And though I shall regret what now I here confess, and cringing turn from this swift lash that o'er my back I send—
I swear that thing called soul had not set torch within the bloodstained walls where creaked my heart, bent on low passion's end.
How could I help but love you, coming like a balmy light into the dead and moonless night of empty years?
You spoke, and I saw the blood of murdered innocence glare red upon my hands, and heard the wailing sea of tears.
You touched my hand, and through my restless life stole scenes of quiet woods and dancing shafts of gold upon the green;
And daffodils and running vines, and larks' and linnets' songs, and the softly sounding lyre of doves perched high unseen.
Things I had dreamed of in my dreaming childhood came again, and solitude with you was what I longed for most;
Out of other distant worlds remembered visions sprang that long ere earthly birth I knew 'mid God's immortal host.
And when I kissed your lips this world was born again, and in the still and starry night I was with you and God;
And truth and mercy bloomed within my soul, and kindly words bred fast upon my lips, and bliss came where I trod.
And long I lay upon the grassy earth, your hand in mine, and listened to your voice that showed the better way;

The Poems of Max Ehrmann

And your own God I learned to love, but loved you more o'er all I ever knew, you who were fated not to stay.
If I am aught, and tired men and weary women know my voice, and smile amid their tears, it is for you;
And if a song has left my lips, some clear and simple song that comfort brings within some lonely heart of rue,
It is not mine, but comes from out the mellow shaded woods of memory now mouldering in the faded past;
And if the springtide and the autumn bring reborn the songs of love, it is because your spirit holds me fast—
Because I pressed my lips to yours in the secret, voiceless woods, where daffodils and running vines forever blow;
And where in tender dreams of waking hours, through all the silent years, my vagrant footsteps often come and go.

On the Shores of the Sky

THE AWAKENING

FROM every village and city and house of the fields, I saw arise a vapor, like the star-dust of the night. And each trembling shaft murmured like running water as it climbed out of the dark world. All else was unchanged; it was the world I had known from childhood.

I also was lifted out of the dark world, and I felt that I was being carried through space, as I had sometimes felt in dreams. High up the sounds of the rising vapor blended, and I heard the symphony of universal love shifting over the cities of the earth.

The music swayed backward and forward and filled the spaces of the sky in diverse running streams, like the currents of the sea. Half asleep I lay on the breathing breast of the music rising, ever rising out of the troubled world below.

The pyramids may have crumbled ere I awoke, and rivers have been born on the bleached earth of dead continents. It was no oblivious sleep, but one that feels itself ever awakening, like the gentle sleep aroused by music in the dawn, or the soft sleep of love that feels the warmth of lips in the twilight.

When I awoke, I saw that the vapor had descended, and that the symphony of universal love filled all the cities of the earth. And I saw a strange race of people —strange with beauty. In the streets men went arm in arm. And there was no haste, and the world was like a garden fanned by perfumed breezes, and the places where men worked were adorned like the palaces of old times, and there was no sorrow anywhere, and no haste there was, only sweet exchange of service, and none cringed, but all walked erect, looking kindly upon one another. But stranger than all else, I saw no sorrow.

I asked, "What year is it?" and I was told. And one said to me, "Thy face is strangely marked." And looking into a glass, I saw that my face had still the lines of sorrow that life had graven there ere I slept, and this I told. But none that stood round me remembered sorrow, save an old man who had had an ancient book in his youth wherein was written of sorrow.

And I saw that the history of the sorrow of the world had faded and was a thing buried in olden times, and I understood then that I had been long asleep. But now the snow of death was melted by love, and as a drowsy swimmer on a sun-kissed beach, I warmed myself, touching this one by the hand, and that one on the lips, to assure myself that I moved not among the visions of my brain, and that the hands and lips were warm.

But it was the earth—the earth of old times! save that the promise of the human heart had been fulfilled. I sank down and prayed, and I should have wept and moistened the ground, but I could not, for tears had faded forever from the earth.

YOU WITH THE STILL SOUL

MAYBE you have a still soul that goes murmurless like the water in the deep of rivers;

And perchance you wander silent amid the din of the world's grinding barter like one journeying in strange lands.

On the Shores of the Sky

You, too, with the still soul, have your mission, for beneath the dashing, noisy waves must ever run the silent waters that give the tide its course.

WHO ENTERETH HERE

(For the Door of Your Dream House.)

WHOE'ER thou art that entereth here,
    Forget the struggling world
And every trembling fear.

Take from thy heart each evil thought,
    And all that selfishness
Within thy life hath wrought.

For once inside this place thou'lt find
    No barter, servant's fear,
Nor master's voice unkind.

Here all are kin of God above—
    Thou, too, dear heart; and here
The rule of life is love.

TO A SOLITARY

HOW often have I unpacked my heart under the stars, careless of the swift night hours, and scornful of the days and years as they passed the horizon of the present!

Why did I not disembosom myself to one who could understand, instead of carrying the conventional face in the sunlight of many days?

The Poems of Max Ehrmann

I lacked courage, faith; and so was kept from my own by cloistering the inner songs save from the dead ears of the silent night.

The fingers of the gods I found cold, lacking the warmth of human hands, and the voice of the stars in the night—though unforgettable—was still incomplete without the music of human whispers.

In meditation I trod the snow-stained mountains, where the air is chill, unwarmed by human breath; and though my vision widened, the sweet noises of the peopled valley died away, and the songs of love withered on my lips.

I do not counsel you, O solitary! to shun eternally the mountain, and the purer air, and the broader vision, and the prayers by the star-tapers of the night, and the footsteps of God echoing on the mosaic of the inner cathedral.

I do not counsel you to blind the spirit-eyes, impatient to look from the spires of immortality, or to be ignorant of the inarticulate language of the golden worlds that nightly sweep the brooding dome, or never to bathe yourself in the strange solitude of the moon.

I do not counsel you to quench the beacon on the hilltop of your timeless self, or to stop your ears to strains of immortal music. These—all these the sweet people of the valley need, still prostrate in the church of things.

Therefore, O solitary! bring now and then from the mountain your vision, your music, and your light. Set your lamp in the darkened places, and sing in the

On the Shores of the Sky

crowded world the whispered melodies of your better self; re-echo with your own feet the steps of God heard in the inner cathedral, breathe the breath of purer air, and paint on the curtain of daily life your visions of the timeless hour.

Though some understand you not, others will kiss your lips to smiles, and sit with you in the luminous hour, and you shall feel the warmth of strong hands, and the light that is within you shall be like that of a wedding house.

And you, O solitary, shall touch your kin with the naked hand, and blend with the music of the world your spirit songs, and walk attended in the quiet evening over the paths warmed by human steps, knowing the pressure of a woman's hand at dawn—you! Godlike yet human still.

I SEE THERE IS A GOOD DEAL OF GRANDILOQUENCE

I SEE there is a good deal of grandiloquence in my book—my friends and foes have told me.

I think it must be true, for there is a good deal of grandiloquence in me—and in nature also:

I saw a sunset last evening that was a gross imposition upon modesty;

And no artist would have had the hardihood to paint that western sea of flame as it was there painted on the curtain of the coming night.

The Poems *of* Max Ehrmann

THE NOISE OF THE CITY

IF THE noise of the city offend you, go afield, when you may, with the birds and the wild, free life that troubles not;

The growing grain and the placid sky have a kind of voice; and though you are alone, the boundlessness of the universe is with you.

The dream of imperishable passions in old history, the love of mothers for children, and the love of children, born and unborn, and all love, swarm in the soft air, speaking to the inner ear in the still language.

Go afield with the birds and the growing grain and the placid sky, and dream and forget; and you will see that you are changed when you awake and the gleams of the city peep in your twilight returning.

AFIELD

FILLED with dreams and songs and love, I wander afield.

Meditation, softened by the peaceful lands of grain and the illimitable blue sea overhead, draws my heart to my lips as one whose talent is in song.

I yield to the thousand felicities of this transport, like a child led by his father's hand; and no questions darken this day of my content.

On the Shores of the Sky

SOMETHING WILL RISE IN YOU

OCCASIONALLY permit self-abandonment to the caprice of beauty; rush past the sentinel that keeps you in the prisoned city, and live for an hour in the house of the world, acquainting yourself with the still people of the air.

Learn the music of a summer night by the restless wave of the sea, or surrender to the sunlight of an open country where the illimitable sky at last meets to kiss the sweet, green earth, and stay till the crimson shafts burn the western world;

And something will rise in you that is not connected with the tiring routine of your trade—something strange and calm.

THOU MOTHER

DO I but dream, or do I look on thee
   Once more? 'Tis thou, my eyes do not deceive.
Again thou whisperest through the years to me,
   I feel the pressure of thy lips at eve;
Again thy kindly, moistened eyes I see,
   And hear sweet counsel that I should not grieve,
Thy gentle arms around me tight as we
   Rock slow, and I thy sweet caress receive.
Yet oft I see thy face with sorrow wrung,
   Until sometime in fright I scarce believe
That I still dream. The tales when thou wast young,
   Thine own sweet hopes, thy lips, and laughter free,
In some weird way are strangely haunting me.
   Thou mother of my childhood's pleasant days,

The Poems of Max Ehrmann

Still whispering hope and courage through the years,
  In quiet, cooling eve and daylight's rays;
Art thou some happy dream dispelling fears?
  Or dost thou walk indeed along the ways,
And know my joys, and all my inward tears
  That cease to flow when thou dost near me seem?
O let me sleep, thou God, if I but dream!

O SWEET CONTENT!

O SWEET content! where is thy mild abode
  Where I may dwell in endless peace?
Show me the much-sought road
And give the lease.

The answer came, "Then cease to vainly roam
In search of me, for thou wilt find
My quiet, hidden home
Within thy mind."

WILL YOU COME BACK TO ME?

WILL you come back to me,
  My friend,
Where evening's golden shafts still blend
Night's sea—
Will you come back to me?

I need you more with all the years
That come,
Each bringing its fast-growing sum
Of fears.
I need you more with years.

On the Shores of the Sky

Some place you've gone, I know not where.
I bend
My head each stilly night and send
A prayer
To you away somewhere.

And should you hear my voice at last,
Come quick,
Soon will the night be falling thick,
And past
Will be my voice at last.

And once again we'll live in dreams
Of youth.
The tender thoughts of childhood's truth
Our themes
Again shall be in dreams.

Will you in truth then come to me,
My friend,
Where evening's golden shafts still blend
Night's sea—
Will you come back to me?

I SIT AND WAIT

I SIT and wait upon my soul to-night,
   And watch the changing sky,
  The clouds and stars that fly
Within the silent moon's far-reaching light
That glorifies the night.

The Poems of Max Ehrmann

Now would some keen, hard-headed son of trade
   Laugh loud at me, and say,
   "Your soul is gone? which way?
And tell me of what stuff a soul is made.
The thing's no good in trade."

And proud philosophers would hard contend
   To tell me all they knew
   Of souls in me and you;
Forgetting where the lights of heaven blend
And shine, while they contend.

So each one to his wish, and as for me,
   I sit to-night and wait
   In slumb'rous moonlight late,
To feel the freedom of the world in me
Like waves of a shoreless sea.

Far vanished earth, I journey with the dead
   That smile in bliss afar
   On yonder liquid star,
And on and on to ruby worlds of red
From earthly vision fled;

Where lonely faces I have known on earth
   Now smile in endless bliss,
   And fling to me the kiss
Of love, 'mid twilight music soft with mirth
Remembered long ere birth.

And evening gardens built of pleasant thought,
   Where tripping laughters greet
   The timid bridal feet
Of them new-wed to bliss; and sleep is naught
But love subdued and caught.

On the Shores of the Sky

Oh, wake me not! but let me still beguile
  Myself in this sweet sleep,
    As through the world I creep
On nameless wings, and rest myself, and smile—
Let me be dead a while.

THE DAWN

ONE morn I rose and looked upon the world.
"Have I been blind until this hour?" I said.
O'er every trembling leaf the sun had spread,
And was like golden tapestry unfurled;
And as the moments passed more light was hurled
Upon the drinking earth athirst for light;
And I, beholding all this wondrous sight,
Cried out aloud, "O God, I love Thy world!"
And since that waking, often I drink deep
The joy of dawn, and peace abides with me;
And though I know that I again shall see
Dark fear with withered hand approach my sleep,
More sure am I when lonely night shall flee,
At dawn the sun will bring good cheer to me.

ONE WILL PASS THE DOOR

YOUR first duty is to learn to live in the world, for to this you are born.

But, meantime, make for yourself a secret room in the inner house of consciousness, where you may rest from the strain of the world, and disentangle yourself from that which is unworthy of your soul.

The Poems of Max Ehrmann

Into this room let no unsympathetic person enter, for he would laugh at you in the temple of your better self.

Yet, in a long time, perhaps some one who understands will pass the door. And who shall say what your life may be from that hour!

COME, YOU WHO ARE WEARY

COME, you who are weary, and sit in the shadow of my faith; and when you are rested we shall journey together, singing gleefully on the highway, lending many a hand, yet passing ever on and on; and at nightfall, tired and content, we shall light the candles in the house of love, thank God in cheerful words, and lie down to peaceful sleep.

ON A MAY MORNING

I AM the dawn, the whisper of winds, the perfume of morning.

The passing night fondled me, hovering close to me, softly, silently.

The breaking day builds the spirit temple of my joy. I abandon myself!

It seems to me that never before have I walked with the spirit as now, nor overcome space, time, and the elements as I overcome them now.

I would liquefy myself to mingle my substance with the clouds and creep into the crannies of the good-tasting earth.

On the Shores of the Sky

I caress the good-tasting earth—lie upon it for hours, my body at full length. I converse with it; and the language is more articulate than the language of men. It is my mother, and the mother of my sisters and brothers, the grass and the trees, and all breathing and breathless living things—the great mother ever pregnant!

I would comb her hair with my fingers, and dry my lips upon her cheek, and beat her with gentle blows of affection, and press my naked limbs against her.

Insane, egotistical rapture! mirth inspiring!

For a few hours here in the still morning I wash myself clean of civilization, and purge myself of things and the accumulated rubbish of time.

I push back history, dismiss interpreters, and stand erect before the dawn, looking the universe in the face, and asking my own questions.

To-morrow I shall return to the human wheels; but now I defy the world of customs and laws, of sophistry and serfdom; and I yield myself childlike to the light and the air and the sweet-scented dew.

A bird flies through the sky, and I fly with it. I am in each pearl of moisture sparkling in the sun. I lie lazy on the clouds. And I acknowledge my kinship with each wingèd thing.

I see all as one, and nothing repels me, as this new day climbs noiselessly out of the valley of night.

Peace lies over the world and over the world of my soul.

The Poems of Max Ehrmann

NOTHING

"WHAT are you writing?"

I looked up, yet I saw no one. It was near the middle of the night, the room was nearly dark, save the table over which I leaned holding my pen. Was I dreaming? Looking up again, I saw, or thought I saw, the figure of a woman standing in the dim light. Her hair lay over her shoulders, and her face I had seen somewhere.

"What are you writing?"

"A story of perfect love," I answered.

"Lay down your pen and live with me the story you are writing," she said.

"I am ready!" I cried, and arising, I started toward her; but there was nothing there.

A CHILD

SOMEWHERE a child is crying to me—somewhere in the future crying to me, calling me by name, by words of endearment.

I almost see its face, somewhat like my own long ago.

I almost hold it fast to me.

I, almost stretching my arms to take it out of the air, feel anew strange currents of life passing in and out of me.

On the Shores of the Sky

The man in me arises, and I am lifted up by the thought that I shall not die, but live again in these hands that stroke my cheek, and in these lips that mingle their moisture with mine.

I should be silent, but cannot—will not, and am unashamed.

Thus, sitting in the gloaming, I yield to this weird vision of a child—my child crying to me; out of the fathoms of things unformed calling me to take it to myself.

Often have I rocked you in the night, child of my dream, when the stars peeped at us and the earth slept.

Often have I walked with you, holding you by the hand.

And often have you looked into my face, dimming my mind; and the philosophies of ages vanished, and the wonders of science faded, and there was no meaning in the world but love of you.

Thus sitting in the gloaming, I beckon you to come to me, I talk to you, and fondle you, child who is calling me.

ONCE I LIVED ON A HIGH MOUNTAIN

ONCE I lived on a high mountain, dead to the distant world of men, dead to possession of any thing, dead to myself of flesh. The quiet sun attending me by day, made of earth a dome of beaten gold, I wandering always on the top, and looking downward on the world. By night the moon walked with me, my brother of the sky, saying things

The Poems of Max Ehrmann

in a voiceless voice, which I understood. The stars knew me in the night and smiled, children of the house of God playing on the mead of heaven, calling often to each other. Not once saw I God face to face, yet heard Him when I stopped my ears, whispering as does the sea on the bosom of the night. I feared to close my eyes, banishing the world, and call Him to show His face, lest I should die. Yet always by day and night I saw His children of the mead looking down on me, I looking downward on the world. Speaking with no one, human speech I nigh forgot—the sighing seas of God breathing in my breast. All the music of forgotten worlds echoed in my brain; and the unborn children sang, and the dead children sang. But naught could I see save the dome of beaten gold, and the playing babes of the sky, and the sun and the moon. And none would come to touch me, and take me by the human hand, and press me tight in arms that held the warmth of earth as I. I saw naught but eternal things, heard naught but eternal speech; I alone was ephemeral amid these timeless beings. The purity of the mountain top froze the crimson rivers of my flesh; and since I was to die, I longed for mortal kin. The kindly human voice, with the sin of the crowded world, and duty, and toil, and laughter—all called for me to come; and rushing down from the mountain top, I sought again the world of women and men, the warm water of human things touching me on every side. In lane and mart I walked with men; drank from the cup of love till I was subdued with joy, yielding child-like to the manner of the world. Now the mountain top is far away; but the love of dying things is mine, for out of death our love is made; and I am with my kin.

In *the* Gloaming and *the* Night

THE LUMINOUS WORLDS AND THE LOVE OF THE NIGHT

LONG did I believe myself evil because I did not worship according to the fashion.

Long did I walk in the night and look at the stars, questioning my soul, and endeavoring to deliver myself out of the hands of the brass images of the earth.

Now and then a luminous world rent the sky and burst into invisible dust; and then again the still face of the night looked down upon me, a single sand grain on one of the beaches of a million seas.

And after a while a great calm came upon me, and though I know not why, I stretched forth my arms, as if to embrace one I loved, and something within me said, "It is enough."

And the brass images of the earth fell from me, and I was made free as the wind is free, and fearless as the wind is fearless—out of the voice of the luminous worlds and the love of the night.

But thereafter the children of the brass images shook their heads, for they still worshiped the idols of old times.

And when I uttered the arguments of the voice of the luminous worlds and the love of the night, they understood them not.

The Poems of Max Ehrmann

Better should I have known, for the things that are inarticulate cannot be made articulate, and there is no language of the voice of the luminous worlds and the love of the night.

REVELATION

I

ONCE, after long weeks in the dust and heat of the city, in the noisy strife of the crowded world, covered daily with the grime of toil—

Once, I say, I stood in the still night upon the shore of a lake; and for a long time I watched the lurid west. And with my own eyes I saw God painting upon the sky-curtain of the softening dark;

And, after a while, the moon and her brood of stars wandered through the night;

And I said to myself I need no bibles of old revelation; this is revelation; out of this beauty is my faith born.

II

Now that night is passed, and I again hear the noise and feel the grime of the crowded world;

But now I am more patient and longer suffering, for I know that nightly God is painting His revelation on the sky-curtain over the lake where I stood.

And over every lake, and over the crest of every hill, and over the green level of every open field, and if we could but see, over the sky-obscuring houses of every city—is God painting His revelation.

In *the* Gloaming and *the* Night

THE LURE OF THE WORLD

"YOU are going away," she said pensively. "I shall miss you, for you have come so often."

Outside it was dark and winter, the wind howled about the house, scattering the snow off roof and knoll over the desolate frozen streets; the tall, stark trees creaked against the bitter blasts—outside it was dark and winter. "I go to-night," said a voice dead with resignation.

"We have known each other so long that I cannot think how it will be when you are gone. Why don't you stay? You have everything here, friends and home. What else do you want? Can the world out there give you more?"

The wind blew, the night grew darker, the windows rattled in the casements. "I go to-night," the dead voice said.

"I cannot understand. Were our many meetings only a summer's idyl, only a little page in your life's romance? You remember we walked in the woods when the trees were green, the grass soft, and the sky a dome of shining sapphire. Were we not happy? You often told me so. It will be summer again like that. Oh, stay! Hear the moan of the wind; and the world is cold outside. Oh, stay!"

The door opened, the wind howled, the trees creaked, the night was darker, and the dead voice only said, "I go to-night."

Into the dark, with outstretched arms, she cried, "Oh, stay! I cannot understand! I cannot understand!"

And the night wind moaned, "Cannot—cannot understand!"

The Poems of Max Ehrmann

IN THE NIGHT'S MYSTERIOUS STILLNESS

HAVE you ever walked into the still, still night, and sat where you could see the lights dying one by one in the distant city—

Sat until the stars sang to rest the weariness of the world in you—until you lost yourself in dreams on the soft bosom of the night,

And felt again the peace of early youth welling up in you like a fountain of sweet waters—until like a child in the father's arms, you felt unafraid,

And withered memories bloomed again in that inner garden, and little things were forgot in the vast stillness of the glorious growing night,

And the same old ships of gold that sailed over the Pharaohs sailed over you in the same old sea of dark,

And epochs and wars and the myriad passions and loves of the myriad years faded in the infinite peace of the still, still night?

I GO INSIDE AND CLOSE THE DOOR

I GO inside and close the door; the world has beaten me, and the love has passed out of me. I lock the door, and sit thinking of the still woods where I mused in old times, and of the friends and the days that are gone.

I sit thinking of gentle men and women who prowl not about the haunts of trade, thinking of nights of rest

In *the* Gloaming and *the* Night

and peace, so that the love which has passed out of me may return, and the trembling nerves may grow calm, and the world grow sweet again.
Therefore I go inside and close the door.

A FEW HOURS AGO

A FEW hours ago, hot and tired, I was surrounded by the jargon of business, myself a part of it.

Now, somewhere near the middle of the night, I am sitting by an open window.

Everything is still, and the soft night air is cool.

The sky seems very near, and the stars lie over the heavens like fields of daisies stretching on and on.

The moon is passing in and out of the clouds, making a shadow-checkered day of the night, and breaking the sky with shafts of gold.

All silent, the universe is doing its work—beautiful, mysterious, religious!

What was all the jargon about a few hours ago?

I LOOKED OUT AT THE NIGHT

FOR a little while I looked out at the night, my eyes wandering from star to star; and I thought how small are all our cares, and how useless our daily pother!

The Poems of Max Ehrmann

As I sat dreaming, thinking, there arose grimly before me the stern face of duty, eyeing me like some monster from the pit of a nether world.

And for a while there was this conflict within me, the still, sweet face of the night and the stern face of duty—the vision and the world.

I would abandon myself to the still, sweet face; it invites and calms me, like the great quiet that follows the passion storms of love.

But to-morrow the wheels will grind again, and the monster will sit in the high place, lashing the back of the world.

O that we had not made slaves of ourselves, multiplying our homage to custom!

O that we had the virtue to be less civilized! the power to abolish the law—save the law of the soul, to be kind and honest and live plainly!

I look again at the still, sweet face of the night, as if to say adieu; yet I linger and look again and again, loath to go, as a man parting at evening from the woman he loves.

O LONELY WORKERS!

HIDE it as men will, even from themselves, behind the efforts of every man is the vision of a woman;

It looms across the lonely way, and on the background of every evening's twilight,

In *the* Gloaming and *the* Night

When the day's work is done and the worker's heart creeps to his lips and whispers for sweet companionship in the silent hours.

O lonely workers of the world, wandering, plodding, and ever wandering, may the kindly peace of this midsummer night woo you also!

SCORN NOT THE INNER SONG

WHAT dreams of golden lights are these
That steal upon the placid leas
And through your heart
Where passions dart
At day?

What mystic murmurs these you hear
That come and ever more come near
In softest gloom
Of twilight's bloom
At eve?

Are these a premonition rare
Of what the other life so fair
Shall be at last
When this is past
And gone?

Scorn not, therefore, the inner song
The soul sings for itself along
The hastening years
Of many tears
At eve.

The Poems of Max Ehrmann

Nor scorn the peaceful whispers high
That steal across the evening sky
And part your soul
From all the dole
Of day.

AT NIGHTFALL

THOUGH I know I shall sometime no more open my eyes to the night or the day,

I am one who looks at the stars when unchained from the work-bench at nightfall.

They are a sign that I am not ephemeral, nor you, nor you, whoever you are.

The dawn comes and the dark and the sign sparkling in the brooding night forever and forever.

I GO OUT INTO THE NIGHT

I GO out into the night and stretch forth my arms, as if to embrace one I love.

I walk along streets which I have never before trodden, thinking I shall meet some one who is looking for me.

The solace of the stars is sweet, and the stillness has a voice I understand.

It seems to say, "Patience, work, gentleness," and I walk on, still thinking I shall meet some one who is looking for me.

The light in each house tells its little story of rewards.

Weary, surfeited with dreams, and solitary, I fall asleep at last, still thinking some one is looking for me.

In *the* Gloaming and *the* Night

ERE YOU LIE DOWN TO SLEEP

ERE you lie down to sleep in the night, sit still a while, and nurse again to life your gentler self. Forget the restless, noisy spirit of the day, and encourage to speech the soft voices within you that timidly whisper of the peace of the great, still night; and occasionally look out at the quiet stars. The night will soothe you like a tender mother, folding you against her soft bosom, and hiding you from the harm of the world. Though despised and rejected by men in the light of day, the night will not reject you; and in the still of her soft shadows you are free. After the day's struggle, there is no freedom like unfettered thoughts, no sound like the music of silence. And though behind you lies a road of dust and heat, and before you the fear of untried paths, in this brief hour you are master of all highways, and the universe nestles in your soul. Therefore, in the night, sit still a while and dream awake, ere you lie down to sleep.

GOOD NIGHT

GOOD night, thou sweet, old world, good night;
Enfold me in the gentle light
Of other days, when gleams
Of dewy meadows held my dreams;
And quiet walks, as day sank low,
Dispelled each touch of woe.
Let me forget these joys be gone,
But feel them coming on
From out the past, with laughter's cries
And dream-enamored skies
Of old. One hand let me hold tight.
Good night, thou sweet, old world, good night.

The Book of Rebellion

AMERICA

LINCOLN, rise up from out thy tomb to-day,
Thou lover of the lives of common men,
America hath work for thee again.
Here women want in sight of wealth's display,
Man grinds his brother down and holds a sway
As in the times of bloody lash and den,
Save now the flesh is white, not black as then.
In toiling holes young girls grow old, decay.
Though thou art dead, could but thy soul return
In one who loved his fellow-men as thou;
Instead of greed that we might justice learn,
Love character in place of gold as now,
Write far across our native land's sweet soil,
"Here none shall live upon another's toil!"

LAMENTATIONS

O THAT I could sing a song that would soften the heart of the world!

O that I had the art to put emotion into words, and make the pages of my book a living thing!

Impatient I grow at the lethargy of words. I would beat them, prick them with spears, whip them with iron whips, to make them cry out the passion of my soul!

I would let out all the penned-up tumult that tortures me within.

I would deliver the world from the gods of stone and the gods of gold; I would deliver the world from the

The Poems of Max Ehrmann

dead gods of old superstition, more cruel than prisons, and blind—a thousand years blind! I would open the doors and uncivilize mankind.

I would counsel that most things called learning be unlearned, and that most traditions be forgotten. I would proclaim the new wisdom—older than the old—which in the process of civilizing ourselves we have forgotten.

Ten thousand years before great cities stood on this continent, brown men sat peacefully together with women and children, and looked at the stars at night and wondered at the beauty and mystery of trees, and sang love songs to the great God, and believed!

I would abolish the universal mad-house called large cities, turning the giddy inmates into green fields by running waters, teaching them lessons in stillness and placidity.

Nature's laws would I make the rules of virtue. Perversion and unkindness only would I call sin.

O that I could sing a song that would soften the heart of the world, that brother would not stand armed against brother, and sister against sister!

For I myself am weary of battle, and the tenderness I stifle in me may not come to life again.

I would have all men rich in spirit and comfortable in body, for I despise poverty.

I would make love free among men and women, without barter in houses and lands, that no man should

The Book of Rebellion

buy what he could not win, and no woman should sell herself—one man for one woman, distinguishing love from lust. It is the same whether a woman sell herself in or out of the law; or whether a man buy a woman in or out of the law.

I would awaken the sleepers to the glory of the world, the harps that play in every wind-swept forest, the living colors of every nightfall's western sky, the sapphire dome of the days of summer, and the still stars creeping through the ebony of night.

Never in the wild witchery of dream have I seen a world comparable in beauty to this:

The red gold of the west at twilight often with beauty pains my heart, speaking a language like the lure of far-reaching sea waves, or the call of sweet-singing birds at dawn on inland meads.

What more revelation does the world demand? Here is revelation upon revelation!

The book of day and the book of night burst with wonder, testifying that there is more in the world than we, and that we shall yet be other than we are.

O that I could sing a song that would soften the heart of the world!

But I cannot; and my wild cries are a picture that is faded, a harp with loosened chords, a reed that is broken. The fires of my soul turn to ashes upon the page.

The Poems of Max Ehrmann

THE GREATER HEROISM

WORK as if thy task were made for thee;
Be strong as if thou hadst courage,
And charitable as if thou hadst been rewarded;
Remain poor if riches are dishonorable,
And carry poverty with the dignity of virtue.
When others dine sumptuously, eat thy crust;
Let love be thy guide and justice thy God—
Not for thyself alone, but for all men.
Pursuing these things thou wilt be misjudged
And, in the gloaming of thy days, forgotten;
Then, uncomplaining, lie thou down at even,
Cheered by the love in thy heart,
And by the full-grown soul of thy charity;
Then hast thou won the heroic battle,
Yet not stained the sweet earth with blood;
But in the garden of love and sacrifice,
Hast thou planted serenely growing flowers,
That shall still blow when thou dost slumber
In the shadow-land of dreamless sleep.

I WENT INTO A MAGNIFICENT CHURCH

I WENT into a magnificent church in a great city, and I heard the minister tell the people about Christ.

And the longer I listened the more I wondered why the people did not silence him.

For, as I looked about me, I saw them that had crucified Christ, and them that had defamed Him and turned Him out.

The Book of Rebellion

And when I left the church, I went without the city to a wood; and I sat for a long time, thinking of the sweet-souled Christs that had yet to die that love might some day flourish on the earth.

And I remembered how dearly liberty had been bought from the self-righteous masters of each age, who worshiped according to the fashion; and my thoughts were somehow heavy with the sorrow of the world.

And there in the whispering wood, where every leaf was a tongue softly humming the songs of summer, the beauty of the world soon lifted me out of the things of the present, like a melody remembered out of childhood; and there I, too, silently within, prayed that I might at least once in my life boldly strike the iron harpstrings of the heroic.

And soon darkness came on, and the lights of the city looked out into the night; and on my way back, as I went by the magnificent church, it was silent and dark; yet I somehow fancied that I could still hear the minister telling the people about Christ.

And as I turned away from the great stone arches of the magnificent church, now sullenly grand in the mystic glimmer of the night, I remembered that the Son of Man wandered barefoot over the Judean hills, and at night had not where to lay His head.

The Poems of Max Ehrmann

I JOURNEYED FROM UNIVERSITY TO UNIVERSITY

I JOURNEYED from university to university, and I saw everywhere the past rebuilt before the eyes of young men and young women—Egypt, Greece, Rome; language, architecture, laws—saw the earth and sky explained, and the habits of mind and the habits of body—

Everywhere chairs of this and that, largely endowed.

But nowhere saw I a chair of the human heart;

Nowhere a sweet breath to cool the heat of that human slaughter called traffic.

A CERTAIN RICH MAN'S DREAM

HE DREAMED his gardens grand he trod
Till morn. An angel fair from God
He saw nearby the gate
He asked to be his mate.

He told of all who lived by toil
In houses his, on bounteous soil,
And that in trade he led;
And asking then he said:

"I've gained so much of earth, shall I
Not merit heaven when I die?"
"Not so," the angel quoth,
"No man can merit both."

The Book of Rebellion

TO THE MASTERS OF MEN

THEY that toil—
What have they done that they should beg
To work and run by your command?
I cannot understand.

They that toil—
Why do they fear some heartless ill
When you draw near their slavish life,
Bound to unending strife?

They that toil—
Some day they'll know this earth is for
Them too, and lo! who shall withstand
Their loud and fierce command?

They that toil—
They slumber low; but they shall wake
And they shall know their mighty power
In that strange reckoning hour.

They that toil—
God made them, too, with love of life
No less than you—in breaking storms
They'll come in myriad swarms.

Therefore, O
Ye masters all! ere whirlwinds rise
And temples fall, and daylight wane,
On earth let justice reign!

The Poems of Max Ehrmann

THOU THAT ART IDLE BORN

THOU that art idle born—knowest thou the weariness of toil
    When the flesh refuses and cries "no farther,"
    And the soul believes no longer in God,
    And the night and the day are hateful;
    When fear of want knocks ever at the door,
    And evil dreams harass thy midnight sleep?

There are none such, sayest thou,
    O beautiful one that art idle born?
    They are in thy house, in the street, everywhere.
    They adore thee, thy beauty, thy imperious manner,
    Thy placid eyes, and thy careless self-assurance,
    Thy soft white flesh—
    Thou—thou that art idle born!

What great virtue is thine
    That God has so elevated thee
    That men and women and children serve thee,
    Yet thou servest not at all?
    And what great wrong have they done
    Who serve always yet are never served?
    Does God not love them also?

No bitterness to thee that art idle born—
    Only be thou gentle and kind,
    And touch with thy soft hand the leaden brow,
    Grown ill and old in service;
    And with thy beautiful face and thy body,
    And the things that cover thy beautiful body,
    Give thou no offense.

The Book of Rebellion

Soon the shadows gather
>And creep over the garden of thy soul,
>And it grows still with thee,
>Thy memories fading like an evening's twilight,
>And thou sleepest in thy last chamber,
>And the vain flesh is humble—
>Thou—thou that art idle born!

THE ENEMY

FOR a long time one who had seen the spirit told the people about the love of God, inspired hope in their tired souls, and taught them the things that we call the things of the spirit.

His daily bread he earned by whatever there was for his hands to do; for the people, though they took the product of his soul, yet they gave him naught therefor of material things.

And it happened, in the valley where the people lived, that a great storm swept over the fields, destroying the grain; and they that had toiled had nothing for their labors; and the fields stood barren like a desert, and hunger and anguish spread over the valley.

And some of them cried out, "Where was God when the storm raged?" And others said sullenly, "There is no God!" And still others were silent. The most violent said, "Let us punish him who has deceived us, teaching us all these years of the love of God."

And straight they went to the house of him who had seen the spirit, and in anger questioned him; but he made no answer, for sorrow for the people was heavy upon his heart.

And they took him out of his house, and led him to a hill, and slew him, he who had taught them the love of God. And there was rejoicing in the valley that the people should be no more deceived.

SUNDAY NIGHT

BACK to the world to-morrow morn,
   Back to the white-heat world,
To grinding barter, sweat and swirl,
   Back to the lips with anger curled.

I'd linger here in the still, still night,
   With stars in the wondrous sky,
And gentle words, and slowing steps
   Of worshipers going by.

Does life demand so much of food,
   Of costly raiment rare,
That but an hour may be plucked
   From all the days of care?

The world is sold to the mammon god;
   The many serve the few,
And whips crack loud o'er myriad heads
   Each hour to starve or do.

Back to the world to-morrow morn,
   Back to the white-heat world,
To grinding barter, sweat and swirl,
   Back to the lips with anger curled.

The Book of Rebellion

DESIRE

I SAID to my desire, "What wilt thou have? Wilt thou have gold and all the things that can be bought therewith, houses, gardens with great green walls, and the beauties of art?"

My desire made no reply.

"Shall I go with thee on a long journey—to the far seas of Africa, or to the warm sunshine of Italy, or to the cold north and flit with thee over the crystal snows?"

My desire made no reply.

"Ah, fame—wouldst thou have fame—the crook of every knee, the nod of every head, the loud acclaim of thee everywhere?"

Yet made my desire no answer.

"Wouldst thou have love," said I at last, "a woman to hold thee as a god, to look upon thee with spiritual lust, to drain with thee the cup of heaven and the cup of earth, to kiss thee ere thou slumberest, and to wake thee with her lips at dawn?"

My desire said, "I desire nothing, and cannot have it, therefore am I miserable."

HIS LAST TOAST

LET saints declare I shall not dare
    Or burn in the pits of hell.
Let loud men scorn and women mourn
    Whene'er my tale they tell;

The Poems of Max Ehrmann

I cannot stay in the deadened way
  Of narrow, hide-bound creeds;
I'll win the smile that shall beguile
  My heart where'er it leads.

Away with tears and shrinking fears
  That breed from the gossip's tongue.
I'll live to-day in my own way,
  Though night shall see me hung,
And my good name be dragged to shame
  And damned for evermore;
So here's farewell to them that tell
  My tale when all is o'er.

SUICIDE

(Chatterton)

THOU God, I'll speak with Thee as if Thou wert,
  And say this is the last of earth I see.
The night is deadly still, and wandering free
I soon shall send my prisoned soul alert
Upon the air. No more the stinging hurt
Of life, for quickly it is done with me.
My flesh they soon will bear across the lea—
Poor livid flesh, thou art but made of dirt.

The hope to serve that once did smite my lyre
In sweet ambition's sunlit days has fled.
Unsought my roses fade that once were red,
And withered is my garden as by fire.
O thou great God, I have but one desire,
To rest my tortured body with the dead!

The Book of Rebellion

NIGHT MEDITATIONS

THIS beautiful world, set in a heaven of wonders, abounding in the gifts of nature, modeled in the great fancy of some spendthrift god of beauty—this beautiful world! why is it the theatre of man's cruelty?

I looked at the sun this evening as he sank behind the earth, and I wondered if all this bewildering beauty was but to mock the little soul of man; and as I looked again and again, I felt a great tenderness steal upon me like the tenderness of one who loves; and as the darkness succeeded the glaring red of the west, the cares of the world fled from me and sank with the departed sun over the edge of the world.

Yet I fear this tenderness that the twilight wrought in me, for to-morrow in the fierce fight for life it may be the weak place in my armor—and I am condemned to fight upon the street.

Yet not for myself I cry aloud, for I am one who sometimes sits at the feast. But I sit there only in body while my soul refuses to come, awaiting my return by the quiet of the midnight lamp, there to chide me gently for the wasted hours.

But I cry aloud for them in the dark corners of the earth. Great God, are we less than the animals, that the powerful among us should gather and store for days that never come—more than the need of a life of a thousand years? What brute maims and kills his kind for purposes like these?

The Poems of Max Ehrmann

Thou maker of worlds, soften this our life ere we perish. In the clatter of trade thy name is not heard, and thy candle is spent in the darkness of selfish gain. The fires of love are cold, and greed is master of the world. Long have I prayed that thou soften the heart of greed. Now I cry aloud that murdered justice rise like an ugly vision at a feast.

Great God, is it Thy will that the enemies of society shall prosper, and the virtuous and the useful be damned to slavery and want?

Great God, art Thou dead? Or living, is Thy hand palsied—Thou whom we thought so powerful—Thou maker of worlds? Is justice harder to make than a world? I shall remember my question, and Thou wilt answer me at the gate of Paradise.

Or if, after all, this life should be the end, who will requite the toilers in the dark corners of the earth? The faith that Thou wilt yet do justice stays the knife.

My brother, I think of you toiling in the dark corners. How sweet to you must often seem the peace in the gloom of the grave. For in the grave there is no weariness and hard words have lost their sting.

Great God, if Thou hearest our cry, turn not away from us, we are Thy children. The journey is strange and we have lost our way. Some perish in pitfalls, and some of gentle spirit await the call of death. Again, again—oh, soften the heart of greed, and before the rulers of men let rise the pale faces in the dark corners of want!

The Book of Rebellion

THE FOOL AND THE CITY OF CONTENT

THERE was a fool once, and to every one that passed him he said, "Look!" pointing with his finger. But no one saw anything. Yet he continued to point ever more and more urgently.

And after a while a few persons thought he must surely see something, and they stood by him longer than the others, and tried a little to see at what he was pointing.

But most of the people shook their heads and smiled, and after a while no one heeded the fool, and there he stood pointing and hailing each passerby year after year, until he died. And when he was dead, the people in jest made a mound of earth over his grave, to commemorate the fool.

And year after year the tradition of the fool went from father to son until a few generations had passed, when behold! one day a youth stood where the fool had stood, and he looked as his father laughingly pointed as the fool had done;

And the youth cried out, "O father, see!" and the father's face grew solemn, for he likewise saw or thought he saw, and he called to others, and the laughter was hushed, and each beholder called his friends and his kin, and each shuddered as he looked.

And through the city of content there ran a shudder like that which ran through each beholder. But it was too late; and ere long rivers of crimson flowed through the streets, and at noonday it was dark like a starless night, and shrieks of inhuman things rent the silence, and in each house death kissed some one on the lips.

And the fool arose from his tomb and wept for the children of the people he had loved.

MYSELF

ALL the questions have I asked,
All things have I tried;
But nothing satisfied.
"There is no vital task
Except to wait till time has fled
And I am dead,"
I said.

Thus I walked in living death,
Smiled at God's great trick
Of life, till I grew sick
Of smiles; and then in breath
All hot and vile with bitter cry
I prayed that I
Might die.

Back I pushed all human creeds,
Standing lone and nude
With God in solitude,
And lo! from out the weeds
Of human thought I looked in awe,
MYSELF I saw
Was law.

The Book of Rebellion

I STOOD AT THE CROSSING OF TWO STREETS

I STOOD at the crossing of two streets in a great city, and I watched the lines of humanity coming and going.

I stood until my limbs ached, and I grew weary of watching.

It seemed to me that these lines of life moved more quickly all the time.

Nearly every face was hard set, and I remember none that smiled. No calm steps there were, or pleasant exchange of human speech, only a hurrying to and fro;

Some breaking into and through the lines, that they might go the faster.

I wandered away, sick at heart, like a wound-belated soldier crossing a battlefield strewn with dying, or like one passing a mad-house wherein are confined his kinsmen;

And I thought of Dante and his visions.

What to this hurrying mass are the beauties of art and the songs of poets!

What self-forgetful soul shall break the arms that hold o'er these the iron lash of need!

Who shall touch to joy and faith this nervous, fearing race,

And plant again the blooms of love and the dreams of hope!

I wandered away, sick at heart, wondering that this should be the boast of man.

The Poems of Max Ehrmann

I PONDER O'ER LOVE

I PONDER o'er love and o'er death,
O'er fame and unrequited toil,
O'er placid young men and young women
Dreaming in the day of their dreams,
O'er hard-headed men of trade,
And the public cheat held in high esteem,
O'er the patient artist buying with his youth
That which he shall gain in age
But cannot enjoy, the day of pleasure being past;
O'er the young nun, barred from the world,
Yet bound by nature to be still a woman;
I ponder o'er the tragedy of idealists
Living in a world of bog;
O'er ministers grown larger than their doctrine,
O'er the chance-taker who has lost,
And o'er him who has won,
O'er proud, beautiful, idle women,
And humble, ugly, toiling ones,
O'er the tired worker in the shop,
And the master of the shop,
O'er solitary women who sit in gloom,
O'er the bride and the bridegroom
And the secret chamber that is theirs,
O'er the dead love of them that still live,
O'er the mystery of the mother's love,
And the agony of ungrateful children loved,
O'er lonely sailors out at sea,
Ever watching the dead, dead waters,
O'er soul-poisoned kings of nations and gold;
I ponder o'er myself, indifferently just,
Breathless in the roaring sea of time.—

The Book of Rebellion

Let me forgive much, forget more;
Let me close my eyes and fall half asleep,
That the pictures may grow softer and stiller,
And the life, O thou God! again grow gentle.

THE TASK

I

I KNOW I do not understand this world,
This universe of life and growth and death.
I do not damn the Maker, saying still
Within myself that surely all is well.
The myriad stars shine nightly in the sky,
The earth yields forth her budding brood in spring,
And always dawn and noon and dark succeed;
Volcanoes burst and flooding rains descend,
And sprigs shoot forth where barren winter lay;
The piping winds bound through the bending trees,
And withered leaves again return to earth;
Soft lips grow hard and tresses gold turn gray;
Sweet babes are born, and stooping, agéd men
Depart into the soft and silent night.
And not one jot of all this can I change.

II

Nor you, my metaphysics peddling friend,
Explaining how the cosmic wheels go round.
I, too, was once a trader in that junk,
And oft have strutted in the lecture room,
Showing all my choicest wares to students bland:
Kant's *Dinge an sich* I doled in precious lots
To scholars, in return for which they gave
A year of nightly brooding, swearing still

The Poems of Max Ehrmann

'Twas worth the price to be so well equipped
For life. (I know they cursed me later on,
As I my pompous masters, too, have cursed.)
And gloomy Schopenhauer's raging *Will*
I crammed into the throats of sweet young men;
And all the other tribes of babbling seers
I sold with profit to myself, until
At last my heart awoke and called me fool—
Called me fool, for I had seen how each
By reason stoutly contradicted each;
Saw the world submerged in theories wild,
Saw all things proven which men pleased to think,
Until my mind in contradiction fell.
But o'er the dreams of philosophic seers,
I heard with certain ear the moaning cries
That burst from out the souls of human want.
These alone, when all else failed, were real!

III

And you, my dealers in theology,
Forgetting all the Christs that tread the earth,
And calling loud for patrons everywhere,
Know you the chambers in the house of God?
Just how He made the thing and of what stuff?
With Christ have you walked through the pits of hell?
And do you know the souls of mortals doomed?
Who told you all the secret ways of God,
That you may dole the keys of paradise
To them that buy in fear your ragged wares?
Back to the vales of darkness all ye mongers
That steal of earth its joy, and fill the world
With midnight mists of ignorance and fear!
With all your wisdom not a raindrop more
Nor less shall fall to quench the thirst of earth.

The Book of Rebellion

IV

Amid the pedantry of mountebanks,
Parading wrathful gods with hornéd heads,
The silent universe goes on its way,
Scornful of twaddling bugs' sophistic lore.
The myriad stars shine nightly in the sky,
The earth yields forth her budding brood in spring;
All nature moves as by a hand unseen.
And not one jot of all this can I change,
Nor you, my mortal friend, whoe'er you are.
Ignorant am I of cosmic things,
And you, and ignorant shall ever be.
But we are not forlorn in wild despair:
We still may turn our eyes across the night,
All lustrous in the gold of other worlds,
Where seas of dark reach on to seas of dawn,
And whisper to the silent soul within,
That all's in place in this God-impassioned world.

V

But there are things my eyes have often seen
That stop the crimson rivers of the heart,
That cause the breath to halt ere it rush forth
To mingle with the breathings of the world—
Not cosmic things no human hand can change,
Nor tampered history, sacred or profane,
The bouncing ball of babbling pedantry;
But worlds of faces damned ere they did leave
The yielding womb to be despised of men,
Born slaves to know the lash from childhood frail,
And fed into the mouths of mammoth mills
Where Christian lords pile up their godless gold.
What boots the question here of trinity?

The Poems of Max Ehrmann

VI

And I have seen ill-shapen women stare
From sorrow sodden faces early old,
As plodding on to toil they went at dawn,
Still childless, homeless, solitary souls.
Once these were young and sweet to look upon,
And fit for babes to bloom upon their breasts,
Like drowsy roses dewy fresh at dawn.
These oft had whispered prayers for lover's kiss
That's born of righteous love in stilly night,
And dreamed the dream but women understand
Of unborn babes that smiled within their sleep,
Nightly clamoring to be born of them.
Unloved they wandered in a loveless world
To join the women dead from early times,
The helots mute of wanton avarice.
What grief so great to wither in the bud,
And ne'er press tight the moistened lips of love,
To dream of music that one may not hear,
And miss the clinging arms at break of dawn!
And millions yet shall die with withered breasts
Where babes have never touched their tender lips.

VII

And I have heard the cries of younger men
That saw no more the stars above their heads,
Shut ever in by trade's benighting bog—
Young men that still did hold to early dreams,
O'ermatched by them whose cunning had no heart,
And left the prey of human vulture's greed
With saddened eyes that kindly looked at death.
No love's embrace to speed their nightly coming,
Nor children clamoring for sweet caress,

The Book of Rebellion

And claiming yet another fabled story
Ere led by gentle hands to dreamland's door;
Lonely followers of goodness still,
Though laughed to scorn by them whom they did serve.
What earthly captain with his spoils of trade
Shall right the wrongs of these that lie so still,
If God perchance forget again to touch
To conscious life these earthly scar-marked souls,
And light again the citadels of thought?
O who will close the wounds of these that fell
Before the piping spears of avarice?

VIII

And here and there, I know, the sweet green earth,
Where now some quiet planter turns the soil,
Shall once again be wet with human blood;
And oft again the knife shall deftly rise
To strike a brother down in godless wars,
And children weep again o'er grassy mounds,
And stooping women, from whose face the rose
Has fled, shall think again of early love;
And younger women dream what might have been.
And all for what? That traffic patriots
May wreck for profit's sake the weaker nations.
O profit, crowned on high as earthly king,
Stretching thy blood-stained hand across the world,
Well armed with Bible, rum and edgéd blade,
To thee a life is but a leaf of grass;
Thy ears are deaf to stunted children's wails,
And dumb thy palsied tongue to mercy's word!
Thou soulless low-browed god of gloated gold,
When shall we shake thee off, and once again
Build up the kingdom of the human heart!

The Poems of Max Ehrmann

IX

The fight to live is now with man, not nature.
The goodly earth yields but by touch of hand
Enough for all. But o'er the bloom of fields,
And treasures hid deep down, and useful craft,
The misered hand of greed crawls in the night;
And all the air is charged with words of gain,
From trader's shop unto the thrones of art.
The smell of profit clings e'en to the God
That men implore and barter with in prayer,
And all who breathe must breathe this chargéd fume.
Thus millions wither ere the noon of life
And die in soul long ere we bury them.
The rushing steps that move in crowded marts
Go not of choice, but driven by the lash,
And dare not pause lest they be trampled down.

X

Here, then, abides the work of wakened man;
To break the chains that would a brother bind,
And stay the misered hand that now is full,
To draw grim profit's heel from childhood frail,
And loose the women slaves in holes of hell,
To lift the human heart from graves of gold,
And knock unceasingly on temple doors
Where feeble souls have slumbered long,
To plant a rose in every barren breast,
And in the din and tumult of the world
To sing and teach and live the things of love.

XI

The sunshine calmly paints its twilight hues
Each day in still extremities of earth;

The Book of Rebellion

And nowhere blooms a leaf but speaks of love;
The stars fret not aglow in mellow night,
And soft peep forth like village lights at eve;
The forest winds resound the melodies
That live alone in quiet, wooded worlds;
O'er ragged mountains, plains and lapping seas,
The silent ships float on the soundless wave;
The nightingale still spends his only song
In noon of night; and wander birds still rove,
As in the olden times, each with his mate;
The quiet moonlight tiptoes o'er the earth,
Like playful water on a sandy beach;
And wandering in its noiseless path of gold
Arises olden bliss we knew ere birth,
And silent robes of beauty deck the world,
From tender leaf to twilight's quiet stars.—
O lift us up, thou God of all, to love,
Above the soulless martyrdom of things!
The rushing world is hungry at the heart.

In the Garden *of* Love

ONE OF LONG AGO

Hast never sat with sadness in the stilly, stilly night,
When all the dancing day's bright beams of sun had gone to flight,
And through the pulseless falling dark a luring wind sang low
The music that the stars march to so silently and slow?

Hast never sat and thought of one, 'mid sad old memory's tears,—
One who had lived within your heart through all the joyous years?
'Tis sweet this sadness that comes on when night begins to fall,
And spreads its silent softening dark through chamber doors and hall.

It is the only heritage that time has left me now;
And on its steady course it keeps my vessel's shattered prow.
And thus in corners of each life you'll find some hidden face
That through the years keeps marching on and holds each soul in place.

So let the night grow thicker still and breezes turn to storm,
There's armored safe within my heart and free from earthly harm
This smiling face of one who looks into my eyes e'en now,
While through the world I go alone till snow lies on my brow.

The Poems of Max Ehrmann

TO BE WITH YOU

To be with you this evening, rarest of the evenings all,
And listen to the whispering leaves and to the night bird's call,
The silvery moonlight on your face—
To be with you in some still place.

To be somewhere alone with you and watch the myriad stars,
Far golden worlds beyond the noisy earth's unkindly jars,
As quietly they sail night's sea
Above the world and you and me.

To be with you somewhere within this evening's mystic shade,
To hear your plans and hopes and tell you mine, all unafraid
That you'd forget to hold them dear,
When I'm away and you're not here.

To be with you and listen to the harp of summer's breeze,
Alone with night and wavering stars, beneath the lisping trees,
To feel the cool of falling dew—
To be somewhere alone with you.

To be with you this evening, rarest of the evenings all,
And listen to the whispering leaves and to the night bird's call,
The silvery moonlight on your face—
To be with you in some still place.

In the Garden of Love

A MAN AND A WOMAN

A MAN and a woman once walked in the evening to a wood, that the trees might hide them from the light.

Far into the deep shadows wandered they, when one said, in fear, "Let us return." It does not matter which one said it.

Still they wandered in the dark, watching the light within themselves, as it glowed in the garden of their love.

The night came over the world and the wood; and seeing they had tarried too long, they determined to return at dawn.

But—it is an odd story—do you know, it never again grew morning in that wood?

AT THE DANCE

WE circled oft the hall in varying motions,
    And talked, through all the music wrought,
Of friends and dress and common things;
    But here is the speech I thought:

"Before the night has yielded all its music
    And the dance is o'er and dawn is here,
And the dream waltz plays as each sleeps on,
    Oh, say you love me, dear!

The Poems of Max Ehrmann

"I hold you near to me; you are my captive;
   And the mellow night is full of dew,
And as the winking, sleepy stars
   Wink on, I dance with you.

"Oh, say you love me, dear, while yet the music
   Still trembles through the waves of night,
Your fallen curls creep o'er my face,
   And the house of life is light!

"For o'er and o'er again this evening's dancing
   I'll dance with you in memory's hall,
And feel your whispers on my cheek
   And the rebel curls that fall.

"And when life's lonely way grows hard and narrow,
   And some great lord your hand shall sue,
I'll then remember fondly still
   That I have danced with you."

Instead, we talked of friends and dress and nothings;
   And the silent speech my heart had said
Lay silent still, and the dance wore on,
   Till the dance and night were fled.

WHILE A SEASON CHANGED

WHILE a season changed I lingered in a strange city, filled with men and women and children, just as other cities;

With buildings and trade and the petty histories of each, and the petty histories of families, preserved by word of lips;

In the Garden of Love

With nightly entertainments and spectacles, with actors and orators and pleasant singers, with ministers, with rich and poor, just as other cities;

But all has passed out of me now except the still face of a solitary woman looking at me through the dim years.

WHEN I COME HOME

WHEN I come home will you be there to greet
Me with a smile and outstretched arms,
A heart of quickened beat,
When our eyes meet?

And will you tell me all your thoughts and deeds,
As in the gloaming night again
We take the path that leads
O'er grassy meads?

And as of old will you my grief beguile—
The grief the weary days have brought?
And will you make me smile
With you the while?

And as the mellow years come on, will you
Remember still that love is young
And fresh as morning dew
For me and you?

I'm coming home ere long to you who wait
So patiently as seasons go,
Beside the woodland gate
In evenings late.

The Poems of Max Ehrmann

In fancy's eye a thousand times I see
You there with eager, anxious look
That scans the rolling lea
In search of me.

I see you run into my arms at last,
And feel the tremor of your lips.
The world aside is cast,
And care is past.

I'm coming home ere long to you who wait
So patiently as seasons go,
Beside the woodland gate
In evenings late.

SONG

THE night is here and through the sky the stars are creeping;
  The tired day has closed its door;
My heart is sad and I am weeping,
  I see her face no more.

"O stars," I cry, "send out within your golden gleaming
  This message to my only love.
Perhaps she, too, is sitting dreaming,
  With eyes that look above:

"Oh, here, dear heart, how oft I've sat in summer weather,
  Alone with stars and dreams of you!
The stars will bring us yet together,
  Like dawn that's kissed with dew.

"Although I know my wild heart's savage love will soften,
  None other shall I ever woo,
And in the starry night yet often
  I'll breathe a prayer to you."

In the Garden of Love

AFTER THE DAY

DRAW your chair beside me here,
As in other times, my dear;
Do not talk or even smile,
Sit in silence for a while;
Sweet contentment over all,
As the shadows on us fall.
'Tis the best of all my life,
After each day's toil and strife,
In the time of night and dew,
Thus to sit alone with you.

LET PASS

LET pass, dear heart, let pass
This pain, this brief distress that grieves thee so—
These unkind words, and doubtful, glancing eyes,
In which till now had shone but kindly looks;
I say let pass the talk of talkers all.
Not one still star of all the night knows aught
Of their ill words, nor does the growing green
In stilly woods where plays the summer sun,
Nor shall the days that come to thee anon,
Nor shall the gentle rain of summers nigh,
Nor olden paths that sweetly greet thy feet.
Thy soul's deep purposes they do not know;
Or knowing, still they could not understand.
Keep thou yet on the way thou lovest best,
For none of all the world knows it as thou,
And all the precious facts that are thy life.
Therefore, this brief distress that grieves thee so,
Let pass, dear heart, let pass.

The Poems of Max Ehrmann

THE DEAD WIFE

O THOU whose lips I've pressed in hush of night,
Whose tiny hand has trembled in my own
Beneath the talking boughs the wind has blown,
Hid snugly from the evening's starry light—
O thou, my all, why hast thou quit my sight?
Thy straggling curls will no more touch my cheek,
Thy voice and smile are gone where'er I seek
With watchful eyes and my strong passion's might.
If all my soul's deep grief thou now dost see,
If thou dost know the lonely inward tears
My heart hath shed along the saddened years,
Break through thy silent doors to life and me,
Who hourly watch and wait with trembling fears,
Lest in the realm of death I know not thee.

LOVE SOME ONE

LOVE some one—in God's name love some one—for this is the bread of the inner life, without which a part of you will starve and die; and though you feel you must be stern, even hard, in your life of affairs, make for yourself at least a little corner, somewhere in the great world, where you may unbosom and be kind.

The Crowded World

THE CROWDED WORLD

DEPART from me ye who are weary and heavy laden, for I am turmoil and distress. Who seeketh gold and the plaudits of men will find them in me, but who seeketh the things of the spirit will not find them in me. I am the battleground and the battle, the thunder of war, the cry of children. Who goeth in me must hasten and not tarry, for I am the riot of men. Towers of Babel build I, yet warm no hearth-stone for the human heart. I am careless of life, and whosoever looketh upward shall not long abide in me; for I am turmoil and distress and the riot of men.

THE PARABLE OF THE SEA

HE PUSHED his boat from the shore and laughed with the laughter of the sea. No desire of the sky was in his heart, only a strong man's love for the game of the lapping wave.

And playful was the sea as a tigress with her cub; but he had known the teeth of angry waves, and he kept his eyes over the water.

And as the gentle rocking changed to moving hills and valleys, and as the salt spray washed his face, and the lisp and swish of the sea turned to groans, still kept he his eyes over the water.

And then, as if determined to embrace him, the monster angry grew; with frothy tendrils yearning up the sides of his boat; and the symphony of the sea broke loose

The Poems of Max Ehrmann

like the grating of the gates of hell; and a whir was in the wind; and a rain arose out of the sea; and he kept his eyes over the water.

And after many strokes he reached the shore; and he laughed at the sea, and laughed over his triumph, for the frothy tendrils still yearned up the rocks where he bound fast his boat.

And soon the whir went out of the wind, and the moving hills and valleys of the sea turned to still meadows, and peace lay over the water, and the sea waited.

Then came forth another, a youth; and he lay in his bark that rocked nimbly with the rocking of the waves; and he rested and dreamed and, as the twilight turned to night, looked often at the stars, fashioning out of his desire a temple for the heart of man.

The gentle swells murmured, singing to rest his soul, and filling with music the temple of his dream; and as time passed on he looked ever longer toward the sky and the stars.

At last the murmuring sea, singing to rest his soul, and filling with music the temple of his dream, took him to herself, caressing him tenderly, kissing his cheek and stroking softly his body; and the foam of the sea was in his hair, and a weed of the sea lay on his breast.

Then the sea ceased to murmur and gurgle and lisp and lap; and the stillness lying over the water was as a prayer; and the people of the sea gathered round him, and the universe was still as it was before time, and the sea waited.

The Crowded World

THERE WAS A YOUNG ARTIST

THERE was a young artist once, and his heart was filled with love, and truth was on his lips, and he sought to do men good.

He painted a picture called "The Love of the World"; but before he had finished, he sat often with hunger and went clad in the garments of want.

At last the picture was finished, but there was no one to requite him either in love or gold.

His friends knew he was only one of them, and they were sure he was not a great artist; and strangers knew not of him.

And soon want laid its hand upon him, and the love in his heart turned to hate, and the truth on his lips turned to lies;

For the God he had worshipped and trusted and leaned upon was dead or had forsaken him;

And out of desperation he painted another picture, and also called it "The Love of the World," but in his heart he knew it was "The Hate of the World."

But the lie was caught up by the people, and strangers came, and he had food and wherewith to clothe himself, and years went on, and he prospered.

Only a spark of the early artist lived in his heart; and often when he stood before the picture in the house of him who had bought it, he looked cautiously about, and if alone, drew himself up erect, and pronounced aloud the words, "The Hate of the World."

The Poems of Max Ehrmann

And once standing so, and pronouncing the words aloud, he was overheard by his friend who had purchased the picture.

And his friend besought him to speak the words no more, lest he be overheard, and the picture become valueless.

But ever thereafter the owner himself saw "The Hate of the World" when he stood before the picture; and once he likewise pronounced the words aloud as he stood before it.

And he likewise was overheard by a neighbor who chanced to be his guest; and so ere long all the people came to understand that the picture which they had loved was in fact "The Hate of the World."

And each in his time, as he stood before it, pronounced the fatal words; and the people sought out the artist, and demanded to know why he had deceived them.

Then brought he forth his first picture, which was indeed "The Love of the World"; and when he told the people, they laughed at him, and believed him not.

And some were for bruising his flesh, and some for taking his life, and others said, "We will drive him from the city."

And they drove him from the city; and as he passed out the gate, and turned and looked over the buildings and the towers of the temples of justice and of God, he wept; for it was the city of his birth.

And they burned his first picture before his eyes. And the magistrates of the city assembled, and forbade that there be painted any other picture, or carven any statue, lest the people be defiled.

The Crowded World

I KNOW

AND will you put the verse aside
Because you've tried
To all the measure of your strength?
And ask at length,
Why should you follow words like these
Which wish to please?
And are you tired—your courage low?—
I know.

These words are dead, they clothe you not,
Nor fill the lot
Of pressing needs that steal your days
Till evening's rays.
You will not read—nor have the time?
You say I rhyme
With selfishness and pride aglow?
I know.

And true it is these words are dead;
No cloth they spread,
Nor shelter bring to you at night,
Nor gold by light
Of morning when perchance you stray
So still away
From strangers' doors in spirits low—
I know.

The strong man's hopeless work of years,
His inward tears;
The dying youth of her unwooed,
Her solitude;
The broken heart's unseen distress,
Its sleeplessness;
The honored now dishonored so—
I know.

The Poems of Max Ehrmann

Where'er you are, though far or near,
I'd bring you cheer;
And you of full-blown maiden's grace,
And you of face
All warped and drawn in time's caprice,
I'd bring you peace.
In secret longing all you go—
I know.

I've dined in good men's gracious halls;
I've heard the calls
Of lonely fishers where I slept
And waters crept
Along the barren banks of need.
I've piped the reed,
And broken love's sad music low
I know.

To you who walk in shadows dark
And keenly hark
For kindly words if but to live,
Myself I give,
My life and all my heart and hand
Here where I stand.
'Tis thus that both our lives will grow
I know.

I bring but this one common thought
My life has wrought;
That from the dregs of drear despair
Still everywhere
There is a joy I yet may sip—
'Tis comradeship
With all mankind, the high and low
I know.

The Crowded World

O PASSER-BY

O PASSER-BY, O passer-by!
Have you good words of me
Upon your lips as I draw nigh
To you each day?
If so, I ask
That you'd them say,
For soon I'm gone and cannot hear,
So speak the kindly word
I beg, and smile while yet I'm near.
I'd speak to you,
If courage came,
And I quite knew
You'd take the love my heart oft sends,
And give me yours as well.
O passer-by, come, let's be friends!
Life's smiles and tears
And happiness
And childish fears
Are mine, just like your own each day,
(You understand, I know.)
So come and let's be friends, I say.

YOU WHO WRANGLE WITH ME AT THE MART

YOU who see the stern side of me, you who wrangle with me at the mart, discussing prices with me, pro and con—do not condemn me.

I do not condemn you, for you are a chattel like myself, answering the necessities of the day—you who wrangle with me at the mart.

The Poems of Max Ehrmann

Underneath the wrinkled face, you have to me a gentle face, and between the rough words, I hear your other voice—kind and low;

This I shall remember, forgetting all else; for this shall I hear again; and by this, in the glow of another dawn, shall I know you.

BROKEN VETERAN OF COMMERCIAL WARS

AFTER the smoke and roaring and desolation of the battle of middle life,

After long marches and countermarches, privation, dreary, godless skies, and speechless weariness,

After changes and the death of the beloved and all who knew you in your youth,

Will you, broken veteran of commercial wars, turn again to the green fields of your youth?

And though the spoils of war be yours, once more, with the simplicity of childhood, will you plant love in your heart,

Grow gentle and walk again with God over the olden hills and by the still flowing waters,

And be pleased once more to be innocent in your desires and to grow sweetly tender in your heart—you, you, broken veteran of commercial wars?

The Crowded World

A VISIT TO A MAN OF FAME

THUS spoke he:
If you expect perfection in this world, you are condemned. In my youth I saw the golden city of joy just before me—always just before me.

Oh, it was beautiful! It was winter and night was coming on, and a young woman was looking out of a door now and then. A bright fire sparkled and gave life to the room. A baby slept in a white bed; the evening meal was laid. There was a bird in a cage and a dog lying by the fire. I said the woman looked out now and then. Stillness, gentleness, light and warmth breathed through the scene in contrast with the dark and cold outside; and strange, this never, never changed: it was always winter and night was coming on, and always quiet and peaceful, warmth and light, and always a young woman looking out of the door now and then.

And every day I prayed inwardly that I might know the love of this vision; and in my credulous youth I trusted the great God, Him of the sky sown with stars and the sun and the moon.

But I never knew the room and the woman and the child and the cheering glow and the peace. I was always behind the carnival of silver and gold; and who would know love must be in the midst of the carnival, for it is the age of the carnival of silver and gold. And the vision remained the counterfeit coinage of my brain, a lure in the soul, as you poets say, something like music one thinks one hears in the night.

The Poems of Max Ehrmann

Now I am an old man, and now I am in the midst of the carnival of silver and gold, and the dancers dangle round me, and there are women—so many women, good and beautiful; but I have no desire, the fruit of my labor has ripened, but the leaves of the tree of passion are dead; the dream is spent, the heart hunger forgot, and I lie like a shell on the shore of time, awaiting a wave that shall wash me to sea.

TO-MORROW

HOW oft you've said to-morrow
Is time enough to speak a gentle word
To one whose olden friendship time had blurred
And set to naught sweet trysts of other years,
When life and love and faith were pledged with tears
That flowed as others' griefs you heard—
To-morrow you intend to speak the word.

In discontent, to-morrow
Is then the golden day when you have thought
To build the temple which in dreams you'd wrought
So beautiful that agéd men would say
With pride they knew you in their childhood's day.
Though old ambitions come to naught,
To-morrow is the golden time you've thought.

When worn with care, to-morrow
You'll change your course for one which steals away
To quiet lands where cooling shadows stray,
And sunbeams tremble on the placid green,
Far off in some forgotten olden scene;
And there as once you'll rest and play.
To-morrow you are going far away.

The Crowded World

In childhood scenes, to-morrow
With long embrace your heart will melt like snow,
Close by the Mother's heart whose love you know.
Those lips from which the rose is gone will press
Your joyous, tearful cheek with mild caress.
Again she'll speak in accents low.
To-morrow you will kiss the brow of snow.

Art lonely? Then to-morrow
You'll freely yield your aching heart the time
To weave some love romance of purest rhyme.
With throbbing heart at fall of silent night
You'll speed to one who waits by evening light,
With thoughts uplifted and sublime.
To-morrow you will yield your heart the time.

When age has come, to-morrow
You'll speak with God to leave some kindly deeds
Writ by your name that softened selfish creeds
Of man's slow moving love of brotherhood,
That brought new hope to them who near you stood
In life's dark streets or sunlit meads.
To-morrow you'll ask God for better deeds.

To-morrow, O to-morrow!
Fast fall the fading years. A thought, a dream
Of gentle words; of faith and love a theme;
A smile, a step or two, and all is done.
Quick is the veering stream of life full run;
Yet in the crimson west still gleam
To-morrow and to-morrow's endless dream.

The Poems of Max Ehrmann

THE HATE AND THE LOVE OF THE WORLD

I HAVE seen men binding their brothers in chains, and crafty traders reaching for the bread that women and babes lifted to their mouths;

I have seen merciless greed extracting yet the last pittance from the defenseless and weak;

I have seen suffering go unaided, and known the stinging malice of them I loved;

I have heard the iron din of war, and have seen the waxen face of early death;

And I have cried in my heart, "the world is hate!"

I have heard birds calling their mates in the still forests, and insects chirping to their loves in the tangled grass of meadows;

I have seen mothers caressing their babes, and agéd men supporting with devotion the slow steps of stooping women;

I have seen cheerful hearthstones surrounded by laughing children and strong men and sweet women;

I have heard the tender words of lovers in the pure passion of youth;

And I have cried in my heart, "the world is love!"

The Crowded World

OFTEN IN THE CROWDED MART

Though changed as are my songs from youth,
   A voice within my heart still sings,
"Live thou in tenderness and truth,
   And love mankind instead of things."
And often in the crowded mart,
   With wrangling, selfish slaves of men,
These words like some old song will start,
   And bring me to myself again.

IN THE HOSPITAL

No one has come to me to-day,
   And night is almost here;
And as the world grows hard within
   The world without grows dear.

O beautiful world of green and gold,
   Of bloom and blossom gay,
Of laughter, health and perfect sleep,
   O take me back some day!

O take me back! I still am young,
   And still would know the sweet
Of lover's whisper in the dawn,
   When lips on lips shall meet.

I still would hear a woman's voice
   By quiet evening light,
And plans repeated o'er and o'er,
   And last a sweet good-night.

The Poems of Max Ehrmann

O beautiful world of green and gold!
  I now resign to fate,
While evening shadows softly fall,
  And I lie still and wait.

IF YOU HAVE MADE GENTLER THE CHURLISH WORLD

IF YOU have spoken something beautiful,
Or touched the dead canvas to life,
Or made the cold stone to speak—
You who know the secret heart of beauty;
If you have done one thing
That has made gentler the churlish world,
Though mankind pass you by,
And feed and clothe you grudgingly—
Though the world starve you,
And God answer not your nightly prayers,
And you grow old hungering still at heart,
And walk friendless in your way,
And lie down at last forgotten—
If all this befall you who have created beauty,
You shall still leave a bequest to the world
Greater than institutions and rules and commerce;
And by the immutable law of human heart
The God of the universe is your debtor,
If you have made gentler the churlish world.

A TRADESMAN AND A POET

"DO THESE things pay—these poems that you write?"
"Oh! yes, so much I am almost ashamed
Of my reward, so very great it is."

The Crowded World

"Then tell me why you are so poorly dressed?"

"I did not know that I was poorly dressed."

"Indeed you are. And think of how you live.
You should have blooming gardens, houses grand,
If your reward is great as you have said.
I understand you live in three small rooms."

"And that is two too many, I'm afraid."

"You do not travel. Do you travel, sir?"

"Oh! yes, I go each week into the woods,
And often sit upon the river bank."

"You are not loved by any woman, sir;
And have you any children of your own?"

"I love all women, every child is mine."

"Come, come, these poems do not pay, I know."

"Oh! yes, they pay me very well, indeed."

"Then what have you been doing with the pay
Received? Have you some secret investments?"

"Yes, yes! I have some secret investments."

"Oh! that is very different. Oh, yes!"

THE HOUSE OF FORTUNE

IF YOU are young, sympathetic, poor, ambitious and honest, it were easier for you if you had died a babe in your mother's arms.

For the citadels of fortune are climbed by them that ask no question of right and wrong, and are not much moved by the tender touch of love. And this is what is called worldly wisdom.

But you, if you are poor and love your fellow-men, the gilded doorway of the house of fortune is closed to you; and you will look with moistened eyes and hunger in your heart till the evening shadows of your last day, yet will it not open.

And here is the triumph: to stand cheerfully outside and serve, though the coveted doorway open ever and anon to them of lesser virtue; and to grow old meanwhile, with face turned toward the golden west, watching the last sunset, loving, hoping and believing still; and through the shadows of the falling night, to see yet a few of the faces of youth's old dreams still luring us onward and onward.

After all, perhaps this is to have entered the doorway, and to have dwelt in the house of fortune.

AS I RETURNED TO THE DIM OF MY STUDY

YOU pallid-faced person with the book under your arm, you with eyes that look far away, and you with eyes that look in, sitting nightly by your lamp—

You who daily browse in libraries and dusty bookshops—is it an explanation of the cosmic wheels you seek? I, too, with rapture have searched in libraries, touching this volume, scanning that, and pondering long over yet another.

Oh! with what a throbbing heart have I implored the pages to yield their wisdom to me! No speech can explain the unworldly joy that was in me, while I pursued the thoughts of one the world had dubbed an immortal seer.

The Crowded World

And at last, having mastered the thought, I cried to the great God in thanks for my joy. Had He not made me a confidant of His wisdom? Was I not also now a keeper of immortal truth?

How I have walked in the sunlight with an air of superior knowledge, questioning the advantage of further study!

Poor fool!

The awakening—the terrible awakening to find that I had been dreaming day and night for months, to find that my immortal seer was not the only immortal seer, that he was no seer at all, to find that another held the secrets of God whispered from on high!

The second cry of ecstasy was less joyous, the third still less, the fourth still less, until at last there was no more ecstasy, distrust pricking me like a thorn.

But now I know the greater wisdom; for pursuing one night the last pages of the last metaphysician who would teach me what he knew not himself, I heard a child crying in the dark,

And I sought out the child in the dark, and carried it on my shoulder to the love from which it had wandered. And on my return, I passed a house where there was laughter, and music, and dancing;

And farther on, under the light of a lamp, one called me by name, and took my hand, and pressed it in his own, and spoke kindly;

And as I returned to my metaphysician, in the dim of my study, I smiled; for I saw that the thing I sought was in me, and in the child, and in the dancers, and in him who took me by the hand.

Tales

THE OLD MAGNOLIA TREE

(A Tale of South Carolina)

"You want to see some one?" the lady said,
As an old, bent darky lifted up his head
From out his hands; and rising from the door,
Came slowly toward her, for she said no more,
And stopped inside the gate to know his will.
The spacious lawn and house within were still;
For empty was the place, some weeks had passed,
Or maybe months and weeks, since tenants last
Had trod the rooms that now lay grim and bare.
Upon the lawn were trees, palmetto, pear,
And evergreen, and near the fence there stood
An old magnolia tree of scented wood;
Long years the burning Carolina sun
Had met its leaves where boys now men had run.
Deep cracked and old, four mighty pillars sent
Their tops to meet an archéd roof that bent
And leaned. And yet some recent art not mean
With color made the house look bright and clean.
"You want to see some one?" the lady said,
The silvery-haired old negro bowed his head,
And coming near with salutations dumb,
He finally replied, "Ah does, yes um."
And bowing on with many side steps slow
And questioning smiles and trembling voice still low:
"Is you de one dat's gwine to move into
Dis house dat's made so fine, please, Miss, is you?
Ah's lived heah long 'fo' you was born, ah guess—
Please, Miss, de dog a-tryin' tear your dress.
Ah's only lived one place 'cept jes' right heah;

The Poems of Max Ehrmann

Mas' Hambleton fetched me from way down fah
Sabannah rivah—Hambleton—yes um.
Ah watch de chores an' does whatevah come."
The lady was the minister's good wife,
But lately come to guard the spiritual life
That parish held far down the Congaree,
In sunny Carolina, 'mid a sea
Of white-capped cotton fields now fresh o'errun,
Immaculate beneath the Southern sun.
He might stay, the lady said, and do the chores,
And mow the lawn, and mind the outer doors,
And water flowers, and trim the trees, with all
There'd be enough until each evening's fall.
And so he stayed, this darky old, and said
But little as the burning days turned red
In evening's hour, and did his work all well
And kindly, with a mind that did not dwell
In hesitation on the longest task;
Nor for a single half-day's rest did ask,
As months went on in that hot Southern clime,
Until again 'twas cotton picking time.
And now the minister's good wife called him,
As oft, while day at east was growing dim,
And said, "To-morrow rake the leaves to burn,
For now it is the cooler season's turn;
And I think, too, the old magnolia tree
You might cut down, and then you come to me;
And there next spring we'll make a flower bed."
He smiled and bowed, "Yes um, yes um," he said.
He raked the lawn and raked and raked yet more,
Until it looked like one vast velvet floor;
But swung no ax into that dying tree,
And sat beneath its limbs content and free
Till evening late, still humming some old song,

Tales

And thus a week and days soon slipped along.
The minister's good wife called him once more,
And standing in the mighty pillared door,
She said, "You haven't cut that tree down yet—
The old magnolia near the fence; don't let
Me see it there this time to-morrow eve";
And with these earnest words she turned to leave.
"Please, Miss, de ole tree make a lot o' shade
When de sun all day a-shinin' hot an' raid."
"Oh—no, I think not much; fell it to-morrow."
"Yes um," he said, as if his heart knew sorrow.
To-morrows and to-morrows quickly came,
The old magnolia tree still stood the same.
Once it was an ax he lacked, and then
His back was feeble, and he asked again
A few days yet to do the task, and said,
As before, "Yes um," and humbly bowed his head.
And so the torrid Southern summer passed,
And solemn, cooler evenings came at last;
And now the good wife's o'ertaxed patience failed,
And once again the old negro she hailed,
And once again demanded—would he fell
The tree, or would he then and there dare tell
That this command he had no mind to heed,
"It's but an old o'ergrown and dying weed,
I'll have it cut; if you have not the will
Or strength for it, there are some others still.
I'll have it down—to-morrow—by this hour!"
With these sharp words his form began to cower,
And o'er his face now old with years of life
There spread the signs of grieving, inward strife.
"Well, well, and what reply have you?" she said;
The old black man raised up his silvery head,
And turned his kindly eyes upon her face,

The Poems of Max Ehrmann

Where shone the power of that other race.
"Don' talk like dat," and then he paused until
His timid heart was mastered by his will.
"Dem buds now turnin' white an' bloomin', Miss;
An' when de wind it tetch 'em wid a kiss,
Dey smell so sweet. Ah's seed 'em bloom up dah
Along 'fo' you was born or come down heah."
She tossed her head and with a woman's frown,
"To-morrow morn, I say, it shall be down!"
"No, Miss, ma good ole Missus she done plan'
Dat tree when de war was los', an ah—ah can'
Cut ut down. Young Mas' he nevah love young Missus
At furse, she jes' a-grievin' for his kisses.
Bofe pa'nts say dey should marry, an' dey did.
Sometimes young Mas' to Cha'leston goes an' hid
Fu' days, an' half de niggers sta'ts to hunt,
An' den he talks to Miss so cross an' blunt
When he comes back, po' Miss she cry and cry,
An' den get sick till Mas' afeared she die."
Impatient with his tale of times far gone,
The woman raised her hand, yet he went on.
"But when de baby Mary come, young Mas'
He change an' love young Miss and hole her fas'
In bofe his ahms an' kiss her evah day,
An' kiss de lid'le baby, too, an' say
He nevah, nevah know what babies for—
Dat—dat was 'fo' de war—'fo' de war.
An' ole Mas', too, an' good ole Missus bofe,
Dey laugh an' cry wid joy fu' days, and loaf
'Round young Mas' house, an' quarrel wid Ann de nurse,
'Cause each one wan' to hole de baby furse;
An' jump around wid ut an' laugh and dance—
Ole Mas' an' Missus dem—dem young Mas' pa'nts.
Den d'rectly say de war a-gwine come on,

Tales

Ole Mas' an' young Mas' bofe to Cha'leston gone,
A-sayin', 'You take kyar ma babe and Miss,'
An' ride away, an' from dat day to dis
Ah ain't seed him no mo', but ole Mas' he
Come back, a bullet hole shot fru his knee;
An' mos' de heartless niggers runs away
An' leave Miss an' de baby, but ah stay.
De lid'le baby Mary, she grow fas',
An' 'fo' we know free summahs dey done pass,
An' den one night de wind blow fierce and loud.
Dey say de blue-coats heah, a mighty crowd,
Gen' Sherman's ahmy come from up de sea;
De cannons roar, de houses burn, and we—
We scared to deaf—de niggers, whites, an' all;
In fron' de house we hear de devils call,
A-sayin', 'Bu'n ut down and dem inside!'
De barns a-smokin' whah de niggers hide,
De sky all raid wid flames like blood—de shrieks
De women folks a-makin' as dey seeks
To hide—de white an' black, no dif'ence now!
De babe she lay on Miss's breast, her brow
A-burnin' wid de fevah. Now dey come,
Like mad men drunk fu' human blood, an' some
A-wavin' torches run inside de gate,
Ah jumps clean fru de window, an' says, 'Wait!
Dah's a babe inside dat's sick an' nigh to deaf!'
Seem like dat crowd of blue-coats hole dah breaf,
Some come a-runnin' 'round whah ah was sayin'
Ut ovah—ovah 'g'in while dey was stayin'.
One shouts, 'We gwine set all you niggers free!'
Ah shouts, 'Ah is, you needn' stay fu' me!'
Den on ma head a knock—ag'in—once mo',
Ah reels, a-stagg'rin' retch out fu' de do',
An' drap right down and hears ma Massa say,

The Poems of Max Ehrmann

'Take kyar ma babe an' Miss,' an' ride away.
One beside de captain shouts, 'De house! de house!'
'Stan' back!' he say, an' dey was still as a mouse.
An' as ah turn, dah in de torches' light,
Stan' Miss an' de babe, like angels dressed in white;
An' de sound of marchin' seem to die away,
An' da'kness come a-fallin' whah ah lay,
An' seem like summah time a-long ago,
An' winds a-blowin' fru de trees so low,
Like fa' off music from de crooked lane
Whah cabins stand along de fields o' cane,
And whah de niggers dance an' sing an' sing
Till stars a-wavin' an' de valleys ring.
Ah soon wakes up, but de babe she gone to res'
Dat winter night, asleep on Miss's breas'.
We bury her one morn, young Miss an' me,
Dah by de fence whah she could always see
De place her baby Mary sleep so still.
An' when de springtime come ah makes a hill
Besides de grabe; an' Miss, so po' an' white,
She drap a seed, den fol' her hands up tight,
An' raise her eyes to de evenin' sky, an' pray
To herself-like, den aloud an' slow she say,
'Lawd, bring fort' de tender leaf from out de ground,
An' let de years spread branches fa' around,
An' let de tree live on in place de dead.'
She drap her hands, an' dat was all she said.
De years dey come, an' creepin' past dey go,
An' from de seed dat same magnolia grow.
Young Miss she soon turn ole an' put away;
Ah only an' dat tree is heah to stay.
Sometimes it seem to talk; an' evah breeze
At night finds dis ole body on uts knees,
An' dah de sound of whisp'rin' leaves above

Tales

Seem like de voices ole of dem ah love;
An' evah mornin' 'fo' you's up ah hears
De warbler sing so sweet it fetch de tears;
An' in de risin' sunlight of' ah see
Young Miss an' de babe sit dah beneaf dat tree,
An' thinks ah hear young Mas' a-callin' say,
'Take kyar ma babe and Miss!' and ride away."

JEFF

(The Story of a Horse)

A SOUTHERN city on an autumn day—
Ten years and more the war had passed away—
A street where men and loaded wagons stand;
And coming slowly through that street of sand
A load of wood drawn by a horse that's lean
And old. The driver with a savage mien
Now swiftly lashes him, again, again;
He sways as struggling for his life, and then
An agéd darky standing by cries out,
"You stop, white gem'man; Lawd, what you about!
Dat po' ole hoss, he ain' done you no harm."
The angered driver grasps the negro's arm.

Let go ma wrist; don' pull dat way;
You crack ma bones—let go, ah say!
'Cause don' you see ma head is white,
An' ah ain' got no strength to fight
White gem'man; now ah say let go!
Ah tol' you not to whip him so.
Ah seed you do ut of' befo',
A-standin' in ma cabin do',
Until ah is dat ole hoss Jeff,

The Poems of Max Ehrmann

An' all de sense ah got done lef'
Ma head. White gem'man, you can' blame
Ole Jeff, 'cause he is po' an' lame;
An' he can' pull like young hoss kin,
His ribs a-stickin' fru his skin.
What! Does ah know dat hoss's name?
As sho' as ef mine was de same.
A heap o' times ah strides his back,
Long 'fo' he knowd de cruel whip's crack,
An' of' ah rub him till he shine
Wid dapples like a melon rin'.
Dat's ma ole Massa's hoss—dat's Jeff.
De war begin', ole Mas' he lef';
De bugles call, de drums roll on;
Ole Missus cry; an' dey bofe gone,
Ole Mas' an' Jeff a-carryin' him;
Ah watch 'em till ma eyes grow dim.
Den months go by. One day at las'
We gits a letter dat was pass'
Along de line and give to me,
A-sayin' dat ole Massa he
Is gwine to 'rive not fa' away,
An' dat fu' me to come an' stay
Wid him, an' ride as fas' ah kin,
Jes' like a race hoss gwine to win.
De letter make po' Missus cry.
Dat's all it say, 'cept jes' "Good-bye."
Po' Missus fearin' dat he lay
Wid fevah, sent me off dat day;
A-sayin', "Go, now go as fas'
As wind, till you fin' him at las',
An' stay until de war is fru;
Don' come back 'lone, ah say to you!"
Away till da'k, an' nevah slow,

Tales

Ah ride an' ride like winds dat blow;
An' on agin at breakin' day,
Ah nevah stops 'cept to find de way,
An' 'cept when white boys calls to as',
"Say, niggah, whah you ridin' so fas'?"
Ah tells 'em, den ah gallops on
Till da'kness come an' daylight gone.
De evenin' of de second day
Ah finds de place ole Massa say;
But noffin dar 'cept jes' de light
Of stars a-winkin' in de night.
Folks say de army norfward gone;
Ah takes de road at breakin' dawn,
An' swings de reins an' lets 'er go;
Dat hoss do somehow surely know
Ole Massa sent fu' us to come.
We pass de fiel's an' houses, some
Whah lights a-gleamin' seem to say,
"Ride fas' 'cause soon anothah day
Is heah an' you ain' foun' ole Massa!"
Ah tells dat hoss an' he go fassa.
Den soon he stop, fro up his ears;
De furse time in ma life ah hears
De stranges' kind o' poppin' soun'.
Ah swings de reins an' de noise is drown';
But as ah gallop all de while
De soun' gits loudah evah mile,
Jes' pop an' crack an' crash an' pop,
Seems like ut nevah gwine to stop.
Ah hears de cannons roar an' groan,
A terrible loud an' mockin' moan;
Ah sees de smoke rise to de sky,
An' hears de bullets whistlin' by;
Ah pass some men a-runnin' roun'

The Poems of Max Ehrmann

Attendin' wounded on de groun'.
An' den ah 'quired, but none can tell
Me whah Mas' is. Ah's feared he fell
'Fo' now, an' lay among de dead;
'Cause whah ah as' dey shakes dar head.
Ah mounts a hill, an' plain as day
Ah sees de bluecoats an' de gray.
Ah looks fu' Massa dar below,
Whah human bodies seem to flow
In smoke an' flame; an' noise like dat
Ah nevah hears. Some fallin' flat
An' don' git up; de livin' runs
O'er dead an' bleedin', shootin' guns;
An' bullets singin' songs of deaf
Nigh takes away ma stagger'n breaf.
Dar somewhah in dat hell ah knows
Ole Massa is among de foes.
De lines dey swing an' reel an' swing,
De cannons groan, de bullets sing;
An' now de graycoats fallin' back,
Dar flag drap down, an' in dar track
De bluecoats press like flames o' hell
Right o'er de backs of dem dat fell.
An' now de graycoats turn an' rally;
An' down de middle of de valley,
A big white hoss like sto'm winds sail,
Right whah de whizzin' bullets hail
In fron' dat flame-line' road to deaf—
It's Massa on de white hoss Jeff!
He lifts de flag an' sta'ts ahead
Into dat wall of fire an' lead.
De graycoats follow wid a yell;
An' all de roarin' seem like hell
Broke fru de groun'; an' in de smoke

Tales

Dat's red wid flame, at evah stroke
Dat white hoss Jeff crowd on an' on.
He drap to his knees, an' up an' gone,
Again he drap, an' rise de same.
An' now behin' a wall of flame
Seem like a million bluecoats come.
De gray a-drappin' dead an' dumb,
On evah side dey fallin' back,
A-leavin' wounded in dar track;
De bluecoats charge like a hurricane
Right o'er de wounded an' de slain.
An' in dat bloody roar of deaf
Ole Massa wheels around dat Jeff
To save his life, 'cause all is los'.
An' evah ridah on his hoss
Comes up de hill pas' whah ah is,
As 'roun' ma ears de bullets whiz.
Ah mounts ma hoss an' lets 'im go;
An' as ah look aroun' jes' so,
Here comes dat Jeff an' ma ole Massa.
Ah nevah sees a hoss go fassa,
A-leapin', plungin' as he gone,
Jes' pas' ma side, an' on an' on.
Ah spurs ma hoss in dat ride o' deaf,
To keep ma eyes on Mass an' Jeff,
Ole Missus' words, "Stay by his side,"
Ring in ma ear as on ah ride.
An' fru dat fores' we jes' fly,
An' some a-drappin' off to die;
Dar bruisin', grindin' deaf to meet
Beneaf de bluecoat's hosses' feet.
O' fiel's an' fence an' log an' lane
Whah cotton grows an' sugar-cane,
'Neaf trees we dodge each bendin' limb,

The Poems of Max Ehrmann

As fas' ah rides, ma eyes on him
An' dat hoss Jeff, an' on an' on;
Ah looks ag'in an' dey bofe gone.
Dar ain' no time to stop an' fin'
Ole Mass an' Jeff, 'cause jes' behin'
De bluecoats comin' like a cloud
Of flyin' flame an' smoke; an' loud
De raspin' rattle pain ma soul
Fu Jeff an' Massa, gray an' ole.
Ah turns an' turns, but don' see him
An' Jeff no mo,' ma sight grow dim.
A crack—ma arm—ah knows ah's hit!
Ah staggers some, but tight ah sit
An' spurs; fu' miles dey po' de lead
Into our back an' side an' head.
Ah turns to lef' an' down a hill,
An' hides ma hoss inside a mill;
Den waits, an' hears de awful cry
Of all de bluecoats ridin' by.
What ef dey stop, ah holds ma breaf;
Still on dey come in dat ride o' deaf,
But dey don' stop, an' all grow still
'Cept poppin' sounds fa' down de hill.
An' now an' den some stragglers pass,
Until ah surely finks de las'
One gone; an' slowly as de day
Seem like it stealin' fa' away,
An' from de sky de da'kness fall,
A-spreadin' stillness ovah all,
'Cept jes' a mou'nful evenin' breeze,
Ah guides ma hoss back fru de trees;
Ole Missus' words, as on ah ride,
Ring in ma ears, "Stay by his side—
Stay by him till de war is fru,

Tales

Don' come back 'lone, ah say to you."
An' many times on bended knee
Each dead man's face ah search to see
If it ma Massa; till de light
Of day all gone, an' lonesome night
Spread o'er de groun' an' trees about.
An' aftah while de stars come out
All still, jes' like dat dey look down,
An' look an' look upon de groun',
Whah many lays dat long ago
In playful childhood use' to know
Some tendah arms dat held 'em tight
An' lips dat pressed dar own each night.
Ma hoss he stumble 'long de way.
Den jes' dat sudden-like he neigh,
An' neigh ag'in! den evahthing
All still 'cept jes' de wind dat sing.
He stop an' prick his ears up high;
Seem like something is standin' nigh—
A-standin' jes' along our way.
Anothah hoss begins to neigh.
Ah sees dat we ain' all alone,
Ma hoss a-standin' still like stone.
Den gives a lunge an' plunge an' boun',
An' quick as dat drags me aroun'
De trees an' logs, like he ma boss,
An' stops in fron' dat othah hoss.
Dat othah hoss don' make no soun';
His rider flat upon de groun',
De stirrup holdin' one foot fas',
De othah lyin' in de grass.
Ah strikes a match—ah holds ma breaf—
It's Massa an' de white hoss Jeff!
Old Massa's face like wax so white.

The Poems of Max Ehrmann

Ah loads him on dat hoss, an' tight
Ah ties him 'cross his back; den step
By step all fru dat woods we crep',
Jes' like a funeral in de da'k.
De stars look down as if to ha'k
Ag'in an' see what we about.
Long time pass, den de sun come out
An' spread de daylight all 'roun',
As on an' on we homeward boun'.
Ole Missus nearly die. Ole Mass
He laid away. De war gone pas',
An' men don' kill each othah, an'
Jes' poverty is in de lan'.
Ole Missus she done sell nigh all
We got 'cept Jeff. An den one fall
She sell him, too; but ah done keeps
Ma eyes on him dat of'en weeps
When some his owners treats him bad;
An' when dey treats him good ah's glad
Jes' like a chil'. See heah, kin' man,
Dat Jeff hoss done got ole; he can'
Do much mo' work. Ah give you dis
Heah watch fu' him; an' you won' miss
Him none. You will? an' it's a trade?
Lawd, it's de bes' ah evah made!
Same as you loves your chil' or wife,
Ah loves dat hoss jes' like ma life.
Dey all done gone away, you see,
'Cept jes' us two, ole Jeff an' me.
An' ah ain' nevah done agwine
To part from him no mo'. He mine,
Ah his, an' we bofe ole an' bent;
'Fo' long we gwine whah Massa went.

Tales

He led his horse away, and sidewise stepped
And smiled, so happy that he almost wept.
That night he fed him such a meal as fit
The horses of a king, and long did sit
By him and talk of good old times gone past,
And always of the master first and last;
And soon he closed his eyes in sleep, and then
Within his dreams he lived his life again.

Prayers

A PRAYER

LET me do my work each day; and if the darkened hours of despair overcome me, may I not forget the strength that comforted me in the desolation of other times. May I still remember the bright hours that found me walking over the silent hills of my childhood, or dreaming on the margin of the quiet river, when a light glowed within me, and I promised my early God to have courage amid the tempests of the changing years. Spare me from bitterness and from the sharp passions of unguarded moments. May I not forget that poverty and riches are of the spirit. Though the world know me not, may my thoughts and actions be such as shall keep me friendly with myself. Lift my eyes from the earth, and let me not forget the uses of the stars. Forbid that I should judge others, lest I condemn myself. Let me not follow the clamor of the world, but walk calmly in my path. Give me a few friends who will love me for what I am; and keep ever burning before my vagrant steps the kindly light of hope. And though age and infirmity overtake me, and I come not within sight of the castle of my dreams, teach me still to be thankful for life, and for time's olden memories that are good and sweet; and may the evening's twilight find me gentle still.

AN ARTIST'S PRAYER

LORD God, Thou who dost paint with magic touch
The curtains of the soft and silent night,
This gift I ask, that o'er whatever cloth
My brush may glide, now to and fro and round,

The Poems of Max Ehrmann

There will come that which ever pleases Thee;
For surely Thou dost love the good of men.
Help me to make the things that beauty hold
Amid these veering lines and diverse shades,
That cheer will bring to sad and solemn men
And tired women in their dreary haunts,
That youth will not forget on highways hard
With troubled years, when somber night is on,
And when no kindly light leads through the way,
That joy and love may dawn like newborn days
In hearts where long the chambers have been dark.
Let lowly life and dusty daily toil
Come near me evermore and day by day,
That I forget not them that still are kind
Though tried by years of unrequited toil,
Alas! and sometimes want and age and pain.
Let me not love my pictures more than men,
Nor follow the wild lead of some mad dream,
Nor see myself as if above the crowd
Commanding that they all bow low their heads;
Instead, with kindly heart and gentle hand
And smiles upon my face, let me serve them
Whose muscles ache in evening's twilight hour,
While mine in comfort still are fresh and strong.
May all these be not empty, idle words,
But all the burden of my life's sweet task.
And when Thou seest that my work is done,
Let me feel Thy soft evening shadows fall,
As when I climbed into my nursery bed
With childish faith, in time's old long ago;
And let the kiss of peace lie on my lips.

Prayers

AN EASTER PRAYER

RESURRECT Thou the dreams and songs and love that enchanted the garden of my youth, filled with the joys of a thousand hopes in the still morning's twilight, and dawning visions in the shadowed, starry night. As the kindly earth yields forth each spring her budding brood, so in the barren winter of my heart may there bloom again the rose of sweet content.

O'er the din of the world and the strife of men, let rise the symphonies of eternal peace. Resurrect them that slumber in graves of gold; and deliver humanity from those cruel conventions that are but the husks of virtue. Make kindness king, and teach us that good deeds are greater than philosophy. To tired men that daily tread the crowded streets, give Thou a place of sweet repose at night; and fill with love the hearts of lonely women. Bring forth sweet babes from out the arms of each, to light with joy the byways of the earth.

Thou great God, uphold me also in the lonely hour; and though I fall in the din and the dust of the world, resurrect Thou me. Even to the last, turn my hands to kindly service, and part my lips in gleeful songs of love. And in the softly falling dark, when all grows strangely still, may I be glad to have trod the sweet green earth, and known the tender touch of love. Yet may I depart with joy, as one who journeys home at evening.

The Poems of Max Ehrmann

A PRAYER OF SUMMER

O WORLD of green and shafts of golden sun; of nightly, silent, silver moonlight; and the strange songs of lisping winds! O time of dreams, and trysts, and olden memories come to life! Sweet summer, may I sing as thou, for every leaf of thine is pregnant with music in the soft winds, and every rose inspires the tenderness of song. I yield myself to the thousand enchantments of sky and field and wood, and play again like a child on the soft green of the earth. And as the God of the universe has made thee to bloom in tenderness, so also may my heart be softened, and the gardens of my life be made to bloom again.

EVENING SONG

GIVE me to gladly go
  My way
  And say
No word of mine own woe;
  But let me smile each day.

Give me the strength to do
  My task
  I ask;
And that I shall not rue
  The toiler's grimy mask.

Give one loved hand to me,
  And leave
  The eve
All undisturbed as we
  Our strength of souls retrieve.

Prayers

> And lastly give sweet sleep,
> Closed sight,
> No fright
> That fears will o'er me creep;
> And now a sweet good-night.

AN AUTUMN PRAYER

NOW the great green earth has turned to gold; and the fruit is gathered, and the grain is garnered. So may we in the autumn of life, mellowed by experience, grow rich in beauty and service, as the green of the earth and the grain of the field.

SHIPS RETURNING HOME

WE ARE all ships returning home laden with life's experience, memories of work, good times and sorrows, each with his especial cargo;

And it is our common lot to show the marks of the voyage, here a shattered prow, there a patched rigging, and every hulk turned black by the unceasing batter of the restless wave.

May we be thankful for fair weather and smooth seas, and in times of storm have the courage and patience that mark every good mariner;

And, over all, may we have the cheering hope of joyful meetings, as our ship at last drops anchor in the still water of the eternal harbor.

The Poems of Max Ehrmann

THOU WHOM WE CALL GOD

LONG has been the time since I spoke with thee, Thou whom we call God. Now I soften the stern face I carry upon the street as a weapon in the struggle for existence, and I cast out of myself all the evil of the world, all possession, all malice; and I yield up my soul, as a flower lifts its petals in the twilight of morning. Unbind me from the things of the earth, and let me wander through the world like the still stars of the night. Come Thou near to me, as in the olden days when I saw Thee everywhere, in the woods and the sky, and heard Thy voice in the silence of the fields. Take my hand and lead me as my earthly father when my steps were feeble. Warm me as a mother warms her child close to her bosom. Teach me again to love, and make soft my voice with gentle words. As a gardener waters his garden, refresh Thou my soul with tenderness, and bring peace within the troubled household of my heart. Knock at my door in the dead and lonesome night; and as I have need of Thee, send Thou me forth to others who sit with drooping faces at the table of despair and see Thee not. This prayer is born of my need; and if indeed men convince me that Thou art not, and that these words are spoken but to die unheard, yet have I been answered, and shall believe that Thou art—Thou whom we call God.

A WINTER PRAYER

COLD lies the lifeless earth, the birds are gone, and through the naked trees the shrill wind whistles. Though the world outside be chill and dead,

Prayers

may the world within us resound with gleeful songs, and the chambers of our hearts be warm with hope and love. And may many an evening's merriment, beside the hearthstone's cheerful glow, make sweet the passing time.

THE LAST PRAYER

I AM weary lying here so long. Many things that once I thought important do not seem so now. If this is the end of earth for me, I pray I shall have a last conscious moment, in which I may gladly remember that, in the days of my strength, I had had the courage now and then to raise my voice for the right as I saw it; that amid the struggles for the necessities of existence I had had time to record a few moments of spiritual ecstasy; and that in the stern ways of life I had known a little of the tenderness of a woman's love. May these things abide with me; and if in the infinite universe I retain aught of my earthly self, may they remind me that in my feeble way I was one who tried— a lovely memory out of the beautiful earth. Then closing my eyes—consciousness slowly dwindling like a day that is spent—let me fall quietly asleep, a tired child at sundown. Peace.

Confessional

PRELUDE

I AM not making a book that will live or a book that will die. I have no thought whether it will live or die.

I am for my own sake manifesting myself, looking at myself, encouraging and criticising myself.

I see you as you pass on the street, but I do not see the inner chamber where you live—the many colored chamber of the soul.

I think I must be taking an inventory of the chamber of my soul, cataloguing its contents.

Many items I do not set down, for I have not yet full courage; if I set down aught in shame, it will not be in defiance or bravado; it will be to satisfy my honesty.

But most of all would I catalogue the love of my soul; for I do not know but that after a while I may be hard and dead within. Therefore I think it well that I make a record of the love of my soul—

A record that may soften a little the stern world, and abide with me until the evening, when I am worn out, and the world is discharging me from service; the sun gone down, darkness come, and I sit still in the quiet night.

MY NATIVE CITY

I

A LONG walk. Tired and contented. I have been dreaming again. My walk led me upon a hill to the southeast. When at the top, I turned to see some

The Poems of Max Ehrmann

cattle grazing on the wayside—and behold! my native city lay at my feet.

How silent, how small, how secluded! Like a new toy in the grass, or a nest tucked away among the trees of the surrounding valley; or—save for the lines of smoke moving slowly to the north—like a picture hanging in a gallery.

No one was near me, and only a few farmhouses stood in the distance. And I thought and dreamed of the wanderings of men amid the toy-town in the grass, of the desires and hopes that had come and passed in this nest among the trees.

I thought of my own wanderings, and remembered some sleepless hours divine with the music of the night. A thousand memories filled me with the joys of other years—memories of friends changed and gone, and of the dawning sun lighting up the nimble fancy worlds of youth.

I thought I could see the place where two lovers met in the dim past, and out of the kiss of their lips I crawled into the morning of the world—and these poems after me.

Though I did not hear their words, unforgotten is their lover's parley; for ere they knew me, it was I who moved their lips to speech in the still night.

How much history has passed within this small space of earth—of no importance to the world; yet all important the life of each to himself!

How many have lived and toiled and planned here—how many, tired and care-worn, have lain down here to repose at night!

Confessional

How many places where elegance and beauty once reigned have fallen to base uses! and how many, merry with midnight music and the dance, have been lifted into immortal joy, as if death were not!

II

O my native city! thou knowest not how often I have thought of thee when far away. When I have wandered amid other scenes, and other men and women and children have passed by me, fondly have I thought of thee.

The cool shade of thy many trees, and the memory of the gentle river at thy margin, have been a solace to me in strange and distant places.

But thou wilt go on unconcerned as ever when I am gone into the silent land. Soon wilt thou forget that I wandered about thy streets in the shadow of thy buildings. Within thy bosom I lay as a child, have grown to manhood, and shall at last rest in dreamless sleep.

But thou, too, must pass away; and where now is trade and manufacture, God in His time will plant another forest; and it will grow, and no man will know that thou dwelt there.

On new-born branches birds will whisper songs of love, and flowered children of the wilderness will drink the sun-wine, and gloaming eve shall know the wild dove's voice, and this race of hurrying, contentious men shall lie—oh, so still under the grass!

The Poems of Max Ehrmann

So, too, all things shall pass away—I, thou, country, earth, solar systems.

What remains?

I SIT AFRAID

O WORLD, how I have loved you!
And you have stripped me and scourged me;
Yet have I loved you,
And my heart has been full of you.
I hear you say, "Who are you
That we should care for your love?"
I answer, "I am nothing,
But I loved you."
And I answer again, "I am nothing,
But I have reached my hand to the lowest,
And I have sat with want
That the weak might be nourished,
And the lonely filled with love."
Each one of you would I have folded in my arms,
Not in the public place in view of eyes,
But on the unseen path of every day,
For my heart was full of you,
My lips blooming with wild, sweet songs at morn,
And softer strains in evening's twilight hour.
But you stripped me and scourged me.
Now silent I sit afraid.

LIFE

I SAT with the stars on the hill of life
    And looked at the world below.
I ran with the winds where the winds begin
    And followed them where they blow.

Confessional

I lay by the sea on the beaten rock
   And rode on the farthest wave.
I watched by a child on its night of birth
   And followed it to its grave.

The lips with a sting in their passions' press
   Touched mine to my soul within;
I know all the cavernous earthly hells,
   The gold-garnished seats of sin.

And love in the still of the star-flecked night,
   When earth was all strewn with gold,
Has lifted my heart like the chords of song
   Oft sung in the worlds of old.

And though I have not understood all this,
   Made up of a laugh and a wail;
I think that the God of the world knows all,
   And some day will tell the tale.

IN THE MORNING TWILIGHT

HERE I stand watching the dawn. In miniature I am living my whole life over again. Other years flit before me and are gone, like fire-flies in the night. The past marches again through the archway of consciousness, and I stand looking on.

You are marching through this archway—you who sit with me in the evening and think these thoughts after me; you who are old; you with bodily beauty, battling against commerce of the flesh, whether in or out of the law; you ill-formed and unloved person; you, disappointed one, making a sorry figure on the streets of life; you who nervously watch with a hawk's eye the outgoings and incomings of your shop; you criminal

The Poems of Max Ehrmann

awaiting trial; you idler in dandy's attire; you who think yourself learned; and you who know yourself to be ignorant—

You—each of you I know, for each of you has passed through me, as I have passed through you. Each of you is my kin, coming where I came from, going whither I shall go, out of darkness before the morning, back somewhere after the day.

O my friend! you should have seen me playing seriously many parts in the human comedy; you should have seen me puffed up with learning, and stepping the nimble step of fashion, with platitudes and quiet flattery on my lips, wearing the political social smile. (I could do them perfectly.) Long, too, with a sad kind of joy, have I made a specialty of virtue; and then in days of inner flame have I felt in me the passion to swim a sea of lust.

The red weeds of vengeance have poisoned my reason; and the dagger of death has trembled in my hand. I have sat in mighty earthly places with the rulers of men; and silently with seers have I seen this world grow small and dim, as I looked down upon it from the immortal thrones on the mountain tops of greater worlds.

I have worked with my hands day after day, and I know the joy; and I know the numb hell of overwork—the leech at the throat; I have been loved by many children, as if I were their father; and I have been looked upon with suspicion.

There you go—all who have passed in and out me. I know each of you; and as you, singing audibly or

Confessional

inaudibly, passing me on the highway, have nourished me, so would I have you sit and rest yourself in the shadow of my faith. Now in this hour of still dawn would I whisper to you the faith that is in me. I would banish civilization, and turn mankind loose over this emerald field sparkling with dew.

This burst of sunlight out of the east, this mystery of the dawning, has filled me with a new peace, and I lay aside the cares of life and sit with smiling face in the doorway of the world; and the many persons I have been are unified and yield to the world beyond the senses—the world of the soul.

O you who are looking downward with still face, sitting with unlighted candles in the house of life, and you surrounded by the noise of the crowded world with its cruelty and haste, and you unloved one with starving heart, and you who have failed, sitting beside the ashes of grandeur that is past—

You, all of you, shall yet be filled, though I know not how, and the dream shall one day meet you face to face as a thing that is real, and you will embrace it caressingly, as this morning light caresses the waking earth.

EHEU!

I WAS not called for greater tasks than these brief half-born songs;
I was not called to smite the lyre and right a nation's wrongs.
Not even was I bidden touch the finger tips of fame;
But in the eddies of a stream I scrolled my name.

The Poems of Max Ehrmann

Yet you who read perchance in after years by glow of light
In evening still, or by the music of some lonely stream,
Or on some silent, God-lit hill above the noisy world—
To you I whisper love, not fame, was my one dream.

Oh, that in youth but once I could have sung a song that held
The magic music of my soul, which ever upward welled
Against my tuneless lips! I sit alone and know the truth,
With broken harp beside the ashes of my youth.

OUT OF THE DEPTHS

MY LIFE is like a ship that's lost at sea,
A worn-out toy with which no child will play,
The sombre twilight after a rainy day,
A siegéd city that no arms will free,
A lonely hovel on a grassless lea
To which no friendly footsteps wend their way.
I sometimes think I see myself decay,
Like cankered fruit upon a withered tree.
Was that one voice I heard of old a lie,
Some drunken poison in the blood of youth
That made my hope seem like the dawn of truth?
Thou God of my forgotten boyhood, I
Am sick of soul, decaying with each breath,
Like one whose lips have touched the cup of death.

STERILITY

I HAVE been urged to deliver some great work, something with magic that shall set astir the world, and make flow again the dried-up rivers of the heart, some-

Confessional

thing that shall endure and prove my power. But instead I do nothing, and sit whimpering in a corner.

Oh! I have chidden myself and whipped myself, smarting under the lash, like a slave feeling the stripes in his dungeon; but I cannot reach out; my imagination is linked to the rocks, and I cannot break the chain; my will lies ill abed; and desire in me has starved as in a famine.

I spend my days in drudgery, and the endless round of daily duties has calloused my heart. I turn as a wheel and cannot break away from the axis of steel that holds me tight. Song has left me like the foliage of a summer that is past, and memories of olden dreams knock no more at the door of thought.

Oh, who will unchain me from the rocks! Who will set me free and light again the candles in the house of hope! Who will teach me desire and rebuild the enchanted palaces! I am ungathered grain that the frost has nipped, a cloud that sends no rain when the earth is parched.

Oh, how often I have set out with boldness to soar afar in some great task only to return with bleeding breast and broken wing! I was made for small performances, and my ambition is like a child reaching for the sun, or like a wild beast that roams in forsaken lands, contemplating the spires of a dead civilization.

Henceforth, I will shut myself in and be silent. And if no other virtue be mine, this shall I strive to attain: that though I dash yet again and again on the rocks, I utter no more cry; though my soul die, I go as one who lives; though all be taken from me, I abide as one who has; and though my triumphs exist only in the painted world of my brain, I live as if indeed the laurel had pressed my brow, and my song had mingled a little with the music of the world.

THE THINGS OF THE SPIRIT

HAVE I spoken in vain, or has some one somewhere understood me? Have I bared my breast to dead book-shelves, and shall the tenderness that has bloomed in me wither like some wild plant in an unfrequented forest?

The world that passes by me in fevered haste knows me not; nor takes me by the hand, for what shall it profit any man loving only things to be my friend?

Once my poems mingled with the thoughts of two lovers in a wood; and once an old man told me that I had given him courage to live;

And these things have I lovingly nursed in my soul; and as many flowers grow from a single seed, so full a hundred songs have bloomed in me, out of the thought that my task had not been all in vain.

And now I know that the things of the spirit that are given will return sometime—maybe only after long years, but they will return.

Meanwhile you who serve and wait, linger here a moment and rest in the shadow of my faith; for the things I give, you will give to me again—perhaps when I wander lost in the night in the city of strange experience.

Confessional

A PSALM

WHEN I wander in places of greed for gain I have no desire; the grass of the meadow and the stars of the night comfort me. Though darkness overcome me, I shall not despair; the God of my youth still abides with me. He showeth me the palaces of the rich and the haunts of the poor, yet keepeth sweet my soul. When weariness overtakes me, I lie down in slumber, and the peace of the world is upon me. Though poverty abide with me, I pray that courage and gentleness forsake me not. And with all living things out of the earth and out of other worlds I believe I shall grow in the fields of God forever.

I AM OVER ANXIOUS

DAYS and weeks, months and years pass and we grow old; the senses respond more and more slowly to sight and sound, desire withers like a flower out of season, and passion perishes on the snows of many winters.

Hope of grand deeds, like a memory, returns less and less often; and the fine daring of youth lies lifeless in the comfort of some little corner of the world.

Dreams vanish, ambitions are forgotten, and the passion of love warms no more the hearthstones of the human heart.

Melodies pass unheard in the singing winds, and the whispers of evening twilight enchant no more.

O age, where is thy fulfillment of youth!

The Poems of Max Ehrmann

We go out like a candle that is spent, vanish like the waters of a sunken river, and are forgotten like a garment that is cast aside.

If this is all, then life is water that does not quench the thirst, tears that do not unburden the heart. Then the crimson lure in the west at sunset is a lie, and vainly burns the candle in the heart of hope.

But surely this is not all. Every star is a witness that this is not all.

And what if to die is but to awaken out of a dreaming sleep—to awaken in a room with doors that lead to every chamber in the household of the universe, alike to the subterranean caverns of an ant-hill and to the mammoth palaces built on infinitely distant worlds that wander through the night in their luster of gold!

And you who quarrel with me at the market, and contend with me upon the street, you shall see, when I am dead, how still I shall lie, and with what peace my face is composed.

But you shall not see me, for I shall have slipped away.

Oh, I am over anxious to know how I shall conduct myself when I have slipped away—more anxious than how I shall conduct myself to-morrow or the next day!

And though I know not why, I cannot say how sure I am that I shall conduct myself well, and that you will conduct yourself well, and that we shall be satisfied.

Confessional

THE HOUSE INSIDE

I WANDER again inside myself, door after door I open, pass through, and close again slowly, noiselessly.

The outer world I leave behind, I hear no more the noise of the street, and I see no more the sights of daily life.

As I pass from chamber to chamber in the house of my soul, everything becomes more and more quiet. Now I pause a moment in the still room which is not far removed from the inner chamber of the quick of me.

All passion, all desire, all possession are stripped from me; the world of the senses is gone, and a light not of the world but of the inner world guides my steps.

Color and shape are gone; something like music but not music I hear and yet hear not. Something like feeling, but neither of pleasure nor pain, presses gently against me at the heart of myself.

The next chamber and the next, and I stand face to face with the flame, the spirit, the God. It seems to me it must be a chamber of mother-of-pearl, with living iris hues, and a flame of saffron—a still flame of saffron. I tremble, for the house has grown strange to me, and I feel I shall lose my way. I have passed the chambers of human speech and can therefore explain no more save in symbols. I search for symbols.

It seems like a light, a still, warm light with a face in it, the face of the human soul, the face of the faint and changeless smile, noiseless, eternal, gentle, oh! very gentle.

The Poems of Max Ehrmann

This I say, though I have not yet passed the last door. I have lost my way, fear overtakes me, I can remember nothing, it seems that I am sinking, a piercing chill runs through my body, I tremble and shriek inwardly, I retrace my steps, groping in the dark, urging my will as with an iron spear, I hurry out, away, back to the chamber of memory and imagination, back to the world of speech, then out of doors to the world of sight and sound and color.

I lack the full measure of courage, yet I remember that I stood in the ante-chamber of my soul.

THROUGH THE MIST OF THE WORLD

DO NOT think I am one who would cover with sweet speech the tragedies of life.

It seems to me that I have drunk the lees of every poison, and sat at midnight with every woe.

Thrice have I stood on a precipice and looked into the caverns of the nether world, and thrice have been recalled by the voice of a friend.

I have ached in body from toil, and hope has died in me a thousand times.

I walked out in youth with Christ in my soul and was crucified at the first crossing.

Curses have been given me for kindness, and the tongue of hate has mingled my name with poison.

So low has courage ebbed in me that I have asked nothing of the world but a corner in which to breathe and hide my face.

Confessional

Years of patient toil, instead of wealth and the goodwill of friends, brought me want and the sneers of them I loved.

Oh, how I should have joyed in one kind word and the touch of a sympathetic hand!

Sorrow, fear, envy, hate, bitterness, passed in and out of me, like miasmatic fumes from the foul places of the earth.

The God of my youth was dead, and on His grave danced the devils of every sin.

Vulgarity triumphed over gentleness, and the fat tradesman was master of them that are sweet in spirit.

Every ideal I had was the mother of a brood of sorrows, for to follow a vision in a land of bog is death.

And the end of all human effort is as the grass of a forgotten summer.

Yet through the night of this despair again and again have burst the rays of morning.

And in the dim light I have bound the broken chords of life.

Out of the winter of the past have crept the buds of spring, and once again have I planted love in my heart, and therefore found love in others.

The lips of malice have at last whispered a gentle word and courage was born in me again.

Toil, though it brought not what I sought, brought something, and nursed again to life the withered blooms of hope.

The Poems of Max Ehrmann

The dogmas of the world that bound me to pain I cut, as with a knife;

And now I wander freely, taking counsel of my human nature and the love of life, lingering where I will, denying me nothing.

And through the mist of the world I seem to see again the God of my youth; but grown older, gentler, and more compassionate, as I myself am older and more compassionate.

CPSIA information can be obtained
at www.ICGtesting.com
Printed in the USA
LVOW13s2149100618
580280LV00025B/921/P